PRAI

Finishi

"The authors of *Finishing School*, a unique and genuinely helpful guide to actually completing that magnum opus drawing dust on your cluttered desk, help you remember why it is you wanted to write your book and understand the long and challenging work of sustaining a project through pesky blocks, the loss of energy and enthusiasm, the omnipresent fear of not getting it right, and crippling deadline pressure. Tennis and Morton are writers; they feel our pain. More importantly, they get the pleasure of creation and know how to instill it in those who have lost their way. This book helped me."
—**George Hodgman,**
New York Times* bestselling author of *Bettyville

"A must for every writer and artist of any kind, *Finishing School* belongs on the bookshelf right next to Anne Lamott's *Bird by Bird* and Stephen King's *On Writing*. I can't wait to tell every writer I know to buy it."
—**Cole Kazdin,**
four-time Emmy Award–winning television
news producer, writer, and performer

"Cary Tennis and Danelle Morton accomplish something remarkable in *Finishing School*—an actually useful book for writers (or anyone) about how to complete a project and not let their doubts, fears, or anything else interfere with successful completion of an article, a novel, or a dramatic play. And they do it in simple, easy steps that make sense and will resonate with anyone who writes."
—**David Cay Johnston, Pulitzer Prize winner and**
***New York Times* bestselling author**
of *The Making of Donald Trump*

"*Finishing School* is the ideal book for writers who are great at starting things but not so great at completing them. Cary Tennis and Danelle Morton know the reasons a piece of writing, begun with such enthusiasm, can languish on a shelf for years. With wisdom and compassion, they'll inspire you to cross the finish line." —**Sy Safransky, editor and publisher of *The Sun***

"Practical and specific, *Finishing School* guides the writer who needs structure. It is for the writer who has abandoned a dream partway through. 'You did not keep your promise to your story,' the authors say. 'The project becomes your adversary . . . The answer is Finishing School.' For a great many writers, it will be so."
—**Pat Schneider, author of**
Writing Alone and with Others
and founder of Amherst Writers & Artists

"With warmth, humor, and a really personal touch, Tennis and Morton show you how to neutralize the emotional barriers that impede writing—including fear, doubt, and shame—and provide a great plan for the actual writing and finishing of your book. Even if you've read plenty of other creativity books, you'll find lots of great insights here."
—**Hillary Rettig, author of *The 7 Secrets of the Prolific***

"This book insightfully pinpoints the importance of time budgeting and management, and of setting reasonable expectations for completion. . . . Its advice and methodology will be useful for countless writers and would-be writers, and for people wanting to complete unfinished projects of any kind."
—***Publishers Weekly***

Finishing School

The Happy Ending to That Writing Project You Can't Seem to Get Done

By Cary Tennis and Danelle Morton

A TarcherPerigee Book

tarcherperigee

An imprint of Penguin Random House LLC
375 Hudson Street
New York, New York 10014

Most TarcherPerigee books are available at special quantity discounts
for bulk purchase for sales promotions, premiums, fund-raising,
and educational needs. Special books or book excerpts also can be
created to fit specific needs. For details, write: SpecialMarkets@
penguinrandomhouse.com.

ISBN 9780399184703

Printed in the United States of America
1   3   5   7   9   10   8   6   4   2

BOOK DESIGN BY KATY RIEGEL

Contents

Part 5: Finishing

Introduction:
Why We Don't Finish
the Projects We Love

NOT FINISHING A piece of writing can feel like the death of a dream. That bright and beautiful impulse to express something truthful represents the very best in you, the part that wants to connect to other people and share with them how you make sense of the world. Many writers start strong, with big ambitions, but eventually reach a crisis of completion.

Untold numbers of novels, screenplays, and memoirs, begun with hope and a little hubris, lie in envelopes that haven't been opened in years, on dusty shelves in the back corners of seldom-used rooms, in rarely accessed files on computer desktops, and in the far reaches of their creators' minds.

You may unconsciously expect that by ignoring your project you can make it disappear, and that the obligation to complete it will fade. That is not the case. Partially completed novels, short stories, and personal essays seem to become proof of your personal limitations. You did not keep your promise to your story.

As you gradually abandon the effort, as the weeks, months, or years pile up, the project becomes your adversary. When you think of it, you cringe. You start to wonder why you began it in the first place, yet you can't let it go.

It doesn't have to be that way. The answer is Finishing School.

Finishing School restores order to your work. It helps you set aside a realistic number of hours each week and define a task that can be completed in whatever time you have. Every week you finish something and, week by week, you get the project done. Your steady progress restores your interest in the work and your confidence in your talent.

The two authors of this book, Cary Tennis and Danelle Morton, came to Finishing School as writers with very different styles and experiences. Cary started as a music critic and fiction writer and later wrote a popular advice column for Salon.com. Danelle is a journalist who has written fifteen books, most as an uncredited ghostwriter. Both eventually found themselves unable to complete a much-loved project.

For Cary, it was his novel, and for Danelle, it was a book proposal. Cary had worked on his novel fitfully over eighteen years. Danelle had had the idea for the book for two years but had never been able to get the proposal completed. By working the Finishing School method, both, in the space of three months, renewed their energy, restored their interest, and eventually completed what they set out to do.

The mechanism is simple. Finishing School meets once a week for two hours, during which writers identify specific tasks related to their overall goal and map out specific times during the week to accomplish those tasks. Cary invented the Finishing School method and has been teaching it since 2013. Danelle took his class in 2014 with four others: two screenwriters, a novelist, and a woman writing a short memoir.

At the beginning of Danelle's first class with Cary, the students examined their calendars and identified times in the next week when they could commit to writing: say, two hours on Wednesday and a longer stretch on one weekend day. Then they set goals for what they wanted to complete in that amount of time. They were paired up with partners whom they agreed to text the moment they began to write, so they would be accountable to someone for their commitment.

When they met a week later, they did not share the writing they had completed during those seven days, only the experience of trying to write during the scheduled time. Finishing School is not about judging and improving the work; rather it is about doing the work no matter how good or bad the writing seems on a particular day. This is an important distinction. Elsewhere in this book you will read about the dangers and pitfalls of critique groups—how even the best-intentioned remarks can lay waste to months of work. Finishing School is different because it focuses solely on your commitment to write.

As Finishing School got the writers moving again, it also revealed what they hadn't understood about the emotions behind their writer's blocks. When they were not writing, they spent that time abusing themselves for not writing or being terrified about what others might eventually think of their work. The not writing, the related self-abuse, and the confusion about what to do next merged into seemingly insurmountable writer's block.

Finishing School revealed that emotional blocks appeared first as mechanical ones. Writers sabotaged themselves repeatedly to avoid work. They set unrealistic goals, underestimated the time tasks take, and failed to account for how their jobs, their houses, their relationships, and the many machines and pets for which they were responsible competed with the commitment to write. They allowed these things to take their writing time away from them, and then they lost their way.

The plain, nonjudgmental format of Finishing School helps writers get control over their emotional relationship with time and appreciate how their yearning to be judged perfect—and the fear that they will not be—creates doubt, shame, and arrogance. You will soon read about the Six Emotional Pitfalls, but for now, if you've picked up this book, heartsick that you'll never, ever, finish what you started, we want to tell you: don't lose hope.

The Finishing School method doesn't require you to change, to become a better person who is more organized, more disciplined, and has life under control. It asks only that you take a few simple steps. This book first covers obstacles to finishing, both emotional and practical ones. By exploring these issues, you will come to understand some of the reasons why you are not finishing your work.

Those reasons are deeper than a lack of discipline, but this does not mean you have to spend years in psychotherapy. You can learn to acknowledge them when they come up, and keep going. That is the beauty of it. You may be briefly derailed by an emotional pitfall, but with the support of Finishing School you can keep moving at a comfortable pace.

It may take some writers longer than others to finish. So what? Only *you* know when a piece is ready to be shown to an audience. As long as you are showing up for work and grappling with it in all its dimensions, you can remain proud and confident.

Through Finishing School, writers once again experience how truly good it feels to write.

Finishing School

Part 1

The Six Emotional Pitfalls

How We Chose the Six Emotional Pitfalls

Danelle

When Finishing School strips away the excuses and the unreasonable expectations we bring to the act of writing, we see our behavior in stark relief. What is behind the irritation, the clouded thinking, the sudden desire to deviate from the plan? For this book to be helpful to all, and not just for those who want to commit to taking Finishing School classes, we thought we should explore what we have learned about the emotions that prevent people from finishing writing projects.

We have observed some truly astonishing things in Finishing School. We have seen that when people used the simple techniques in this program, the thoughts and feelings that had held them back became transparent to them. People who had been stuck got unstuck. People who had been fearful became confident. People who had been unhappy with their work enjoyed it again. Insights and breakthroughs brought people a lighthearted relief they had not felt in years.

We thought this book should ask why that is so, and offer some answers. We made a list of things we had heard people say, voices and beliefs that tormented them and kept them from finishing. We read the list out loud. It was a little embarrassing at first, saying these things out loud, because they hit home, sometimes uncomfortably so. Once we got going, though, it turned out to be fun. We were shouting out all these awful statements, many of which became chapters in this book.

The next time we met, it was clear that the pages that chronicled this negativity easily divided into six categories: doubt, shame, yearning, fear, judgment, and arrogance.

DOUBT—I can't do this. I'm a terrible writer. No, I'm a good writer, better than most people I know, but I'll never be like Flannery O'Connor. My brain isn't that big and my ideas are not that original. I'll never finish, so why go on?

SHAME—I'm a loser. I never finish anything and now I'm not going to finish this. I'm ashamed to even look at the writing I did two years ago. Everyone knows I'm a loser. Where did I get the idea that anyone would want to read my stupid words?

YEARNING—This has to be perfect and it has to be good enough to make me famous. I'm going to write something beautiful and perfect, and everyone will know that I am perfect too, because this is an expression of me. I cannot make a single mistake. And unless every sentence is perfect, it's not worth doing.

FEAR—If I do finish, it will be a failure. Getting rejected will be so humiliating and discouraging that it's better not even to try. Those people who say what doesn't kill you makes you stronger are liars. What doesn't kill you destroys some piece of you. What doesn't kill you makes you want to go crawl into a hole and never show your face again. If I never finish, at least I've never failed.

JUDGMENT—My writing sucks. I'm scared to let other people read it because I don't want to be found out as the mediocre person I know myself to be. If I finish, I'm going to be the butt of jokes I'll never hear, banned from family gatherings because of the things I wrote about them. When I reveal to others my true self, they will despise me. The idea of sending my work out for sale, or to agents, makes me sick to my stomach.

ARROGANCE—I don't need any help to get things done. I just do it. That's what I do. I get so annoyed by writers' groups, those losers. None of them has ever published anything. I don't want to share the credit, or the pain, with anyone. My pain is so much more exquisite than the pain of losers, because I am not a loser and I do not want their unexceptional support.

After we whittled the list down to six, we decided it was very useful for anyone who wanted to examine the reasons why they had not finished their work. The pitfalls that resonated for Cary were different from those that resonated with me. We found that our students identified with one, two, or three, but not all. Everybody resonated with shame. Cary felt shame, arrogance, and fear; I felt arrogance and judgment, with shame coming in third.

The list helped writers get back to work by making them

understand that they weren't necessarily lazy or undisciplined but were facing big emotional issues when they sat down to write.

Creative people need a way to speak about this without fear. By naming these emotional blocks and exploring them in this book, we hope to take away some of the sting these statements carry, just as we experienced on the day that we exposed to each other our most depressing judgments about ourselves and our work. This is why a significant part of this book is devoted to trying to identify and explore the Six Emotional Pitfalls.

How can identifying them be useful to you? It can help you to be honest about the turmoil the pitfalls cause and to recognize that in this turmoil you are joined by everyone who has ever tried to write. All writers who have written about the difficulty of writing cite these emotions, be they famous and successful or amateurs writing alone and just for themselves. These emotions are real. They reflect the seriousness with which you take the task, but they are not a verdict. They are, like all emotions, something that comes and passes. If you have a way to discuss them, you may find the process of recognizing and releasing them easier, and because of that you will get back to work.

Doubt
"I Think I Can't"

Doubt Masquerading as Self-Knowledge: "I'm a Terrible Writer"

Cary

DO YOU EVER say to yourself, "I'm a terrible writer"?

You just shouldn't say that, because it's not true. It can't be true. Here is why. If you are feeling bad about yourself, fine. I feel bad about myself too. But saying "I'm a terrible writer" is what cognitive therapists call global labeling, or globalizing. It not only isn't true—and that's one good reason not to say it—but it can actually harm you. Cognitive therapists know that the things we say about ourselves affect our moods; saying them can actually affect how we feel and, in a sense, bring about the very things they assert. That is, if you keep saying, "I'm a terrible writer," you will find yourself unable to write and thus will never achieve the thing you want to achieve.

Saying "I'm a terrible writer" can be pretty useful, though, in one sense. It's a great way to avoid feeling things you don't want to feel.

So when you find yourself thinking, "I'm a terrible writer," ask what it is you don't want to feel. Is it the uncertainty of ever attaining your hopes and dreams for yourself as a writer? Is it your fervent but fragile desire to be understood and appreciated for your writing? Is it the particular emotions that come up during your actual writing, feelings that seem like they might get out of control or threaten your secure sense of who you are, what you are worth, and how you look to other people?

Saying "I'm a terrible writer" must serve some purpose. If it didn't matter to you, you wouldn't say anything at all. It's a clear signal that you have some powerful feelings about the issue of your writing.

Well, surprise. Those powerful feelings you have about your writing—those feelings that in the past have stopped you from writing—can actually be used to stimulate some good writing, perhaps the best writing you've done in a long time. Because they're *real* feelings. Real feelings make good writing. That's the simple, honest truth.

So make no mistake: I *am* saying that you shouldn't say, "I'm a terrible writer." You should never say that, because it is masking some other thought or feeling you are having about yourself. If you do say it, here are some of the things you might actually mean:

- I am uncomfortable revealing my true self.
- I want to learn to write better but I fear being judged by others, so I beat them to the punch.
- I'm not sure how to improve, so it seems pointless to begin.
- It's frustrating to do something when I'm not better at it than everyone else.

- I was hurt once by something someone said about my writing and I never forgot it. I don't think about it consciously all that much, though, do I?
- Saying "I'm a terrible writer" has often elicited sympathy and agreement, so it's easier than saying I'd like to improve my writing but don't know how.
- When I say I'm a terrible writer, I actually mean that I feel shame, disgust, hopelessness, fear, and anger too—anger at all those who would critique my writing without giving me concrete suggestions for getting better.

Okay, now try this, just as an experiment. Say to yourself, "I'm a terrible writer." Notice how it feels. What event or experience is flashing through your mind? What do you see? What do you remember?

As writers, we can work with negative statements like that. We can neutralize them by using them as jumping-off points for imaginative and emotional work. We can make good writing out of them.

Write about what it means for you to say, "I am a terrible writer." It might be something someone said about your writing, or getting a bad grade on a report, or whatever. Write about that. Recall it in detail. That memory is yours and yours alone, and it is powerful and worth writing honestly about. If you write honestly, it will not be terrible writing. In writing something that is not terrible, you will have disproved the axiom "I'm a terrible writer."

Maybe you don't want to disprove the axiom. The axiom can get you out of things. Long-term, though, it's stopping you from doing something you want to do.

So write about the event that flashes through your mind when you say, "I'm a terrible writer." Pay attention to what happens as you begin to write about this thing.

You may start to feel drowsy or irritated or frustrated. Maybe that is when the thought comes to mind, "I am a terrible writer."

Keep going. When images come into your head, pay attention to their physical details, the quality of light, the voices. Write it all down. It's material!

No person is free from negative thoughts like these. What makes a writer different from other people is that you can look at a negative thought and make a choice to use it. You can turn it into something. You might attribute it to a fictional character and ask that character, "Why do you say that?" And the character might answer, "I say that because in fifth grade I turned in a paper and it came back with red marks all over it. So, in my fifth-grade mind, I decided I must be a terrible writer."

If you continue to interrogate this character, images may arise. You might imagine the desk of this child and the voice of the teacher and the stuffy air in the classroom and the tears that fell onto the paper, that wide-lined pulpy paper of elementary school. You'll feel the smooth, laminated plywood surface of the metal desk with the compartment underneath. You'll feel how the child sitting at that desk fervently longed to be able to write, how the dream of being able to write hovered over him like a glimmering object just out of reach. In handwriting class, he tried to get the letters right but kept reversing the *P* and the *R*. Some girls in his class had such beautiful handwriting that he wondered how they did it. Their handwriting seemed one with their beauty and their person, and he marveled at their unattainable grace. You'll remember how worried he was that if his parents saw his paper with all the red marks on it, they would think he was screwing up in school. You'll feel the humiliation he anticipated and how he cried when he showed his mother the paper and how his mother was so kind about it. But still, many years later, when the grown man had to write a report for his boss, sometimes he would hear that voice in his head saying, "I'm a terrible writer." He'd look around for someone else who would write it, or he'd delay writing it, or he'd wait until the last minute and then dash something off. After all, he believes deep down he's a terrible writer.

A writer can experience something and then enter into the emotion of it and unpack what is there by following the images that come to mind. This is the great power of being a writer: anything that comes into our heads, however screwed up or crazy it is, can be used as material. We can do this with our very worst secret and most shameful thoughts and feelings. We can attribute them to fictional characters, and if people ask us if they represent us, we can say, "No, of course not. It's fiction."

These thoughts, these awful thoughts that haunt us, we use them as fuel for our work. We burn them up in the furnace of the heart. The memories, the pain, the crazy things that come into our heads—they're all just fuel. We burn them all in the furnace of the heart.

Doubt Clothed in Cynicism: "All My Ideas Are Clichés, but Clichés Sell"

Danelle

MANY PEOPLE SAY they have a book in them, and I believe them. Everyone has lived through at least one time in life that could become a book if they could find the way to tell that story. All you have to do is ask a few questions and it tumbles out, even if you're chatting with strangers. The trouble comes when you try to take it from the perfect way it exists in your mind and get it onto the page. The story may be strong and clear in your head, but when you sit down to write it, the ghosts of dozens of successful novels smother your confidence, and you begin to think that your beautiful idea is a tired cliché.

At a New Year's Day party in 2016, I tried an experiment that demonstrated this, although I didn't intend it to.

I had moved to a new town and wanted to make friends. As I was driving to the party, I tried to think what I could ask people besides where they grew up and what they did for a living. I wanted to come up with a question that would reveal something more. I decided to ask, "Did you ever have a moment when your whole life fell apart?" That's a bold question, so I expected some would refuse to answer, but I knew that those who answered would be more likely to become a friend.

People were not put off by my question, but they answered bluntly, without details: divorce, bankruptcy, death of a friend. As the party progressed, I started to think that the question was not a good one. In my last attempt, I interrupted a man who, if I remember right, was talking about beer.

He paused before he answered, as if he were not sure he wanted to tell me. Then he raised his right arm and pulled back his sleeve to reveal his forearm. The muscle bulged thick at the back of his wrist and swelled broadly at the middle, outsized for his limb.

"This is my thigh muscle," he said. "I was in a car accident that stripped everything to the bone. And I'm a bass player."

I had an impulse to embrace him, because I believed I had felt some of his pain and I wanted to take a bit of it away. The intensity of the moment was uncomfortable. I deflected this genuine connection by starting to describe a car accident in which a friend of mine was almost killed. All I got out of my mouth was, "I have a friend who . . ." The man held up his palm to stop me. "Please," he said. "I can't hear comparisons."

I felt that rebuke, and then I felt the power of his story more strongly. I respected his instinct to protect it. He couldn't bear to have what he had experienced ranked against others' losses. For that reason, he kept a good deal of his story private. Yet he said these three sentences to a stranger because this was a story he still needed to tell.

We come to the craft of writing with this same emotion.

Something happened to us: we witnessed something or observed something that defined us or reordered our world. If we can describe it well, we may illuminate this experience for those who read about it. The story is not like other stories because of what we bring to it, and we want with a full heart to get every detail of it right. This story is our own, but it is not our possession. It is something we ache to give to others because in doing so we can touch another, as that man touched me. Yet often we hear people talk about writing as if it were a gimmick or a racket.

You've heard the people I'm describing here, the ones who scoff at every book on the best-seller list, every author who is a commercial success or has a franchise through which he's published dozens of novels, like James Patterson or perhaps a more high-toned series, such as the novels of Alexander McCall Smith. These cynics say popular books are all crap, just commercial products like every other bastardized commodity produced in corporate America. They look at a ghostwritten memoir of a reality television star, a cheesy self-help book, some noisy spiritual advice from a charlatan that has sat on the best-seller list for ten weeks, as proof that if you want to be a successful writer you have to sell your soul.

The writing cynic speaks about writing in commercial terms, conjecturing how to turn his or her painful breakup into a blockbuster hit. "This could be a great romcom," one might say, using movie slang for a romantic comedy. "Or a thriller or a thriller-romance with a sci-fi twist." They think less about how the story might unfold and more about how to shoehorn it into a genre that has a predictable form. Through that form, they imagine, they will receive a big payoff from a long stay on the best-seller list, the very list they scorned.

This attitude toward writing brings with it a distorted idea of time. These cynics say that because the work they are attempting is formulaic, it shouldn't take much time to get it done. "I'll just bang it out this weekend," I've heard people say. "Strap in and slam it out."

Cynicism is armor to protect the tender spirit from the widespread world of crap. Our daily interactions with mediocrity and manipulation are bound to make us feel that if this is what sells, the effort required to write something good is hardly worth it. The gatekeepers who refuse to publish good writers' work have made huge mistakes that make you question why they hold the power they do. Publishing scandals like James Frey's *A Million Little Pieces* (3.5 million copies sold) and *Three Cups of Tea* by Greg Mortenson (four years on the best-seller list) help make the case for such cynicism. These nonfiction best sellers were later discovered to have significant sections that were wholly made up. The writers lied, and the publishers did not check to ensure that readers were not being scammed by a powerful tale. Pile up these frauds and popularly acclaimed phonies and you have a heap of crap tall enough to justify a dismissive attitude toward those who are idealistic about their writing.

James Frey is a gifted writer, and many parts of *A Million Little Pieces* are quite moving. They would be moving in a novel too. Frey broke trust with his readers when he said all of his story was true. Saying it's nonfiction makes him more of a hero of his story. He's saying he was brave enough not to blink at the terrible things he did, nor to exaggerate for effect. Then he did the opposite. He exaggerated his fall so his recovery would seem more remarkable. As he said in his apology interview with Oprah, who had magnified his success by touting his book in her book club, "I was a bad guy. If I was gonna write a book that was true, and I was gonna write a book that was honest, then I was gonna have to write about myself in very, very negative ways." He did not want to face the truth of who he was, but he wanted to write a best seller. His ambition, his cynicism, and his insecurity met up on the page to create the fraudulent storytelling that eventually produced his downfall. At first I was angry at the contempt he showed for his readers, but then I saw how terrified he was of them.

Ken Kesey wrote about America's fog of cynicism, our lost belief that anything can be true or good. And although Kesey was writing decades ago, that fog seems only to have thickened. Our world numbs us with its superficiality and speed, making all of us, no matter how young and beautiful, feel that we are out of date and being left behind. Value is something established in the marketplace rather than something that reflects our principles, and this makes us feel that what we value is worthless if the marketplace doesn't value it too. Cynically bad-mouthing the business of publishing may make a writer temporarily feel superior, unable to be fooled. But this knowing attitude is a thin cover for an underlying tenderness the writer is struggling to find the words to express.

When the cynic discovers that writing the truth is harder than imagined, denigrating publishing becomes an attractive way of avoiding the work ahead.

If you have this attitude, you will never finish. Contempt for the work does not motivate you to work. If you think this way as you write, you are essentially doing it because it's not worth doing. If you are going to keep going, you've got to love the work, the thing itself, and all it is putting you through. There are no shortcuts through this process, and cynicism is a waste of your time.

The man at the party was the opposite of cynical about telling his story. He had reduced it to its essence and left enormous space around it by saying it so simply. In those three sentences, he described a whole world. Everyone near him when he pulled up his sleeve at that party rushed forward to feel his loss, as they had felt many of their own. In this way, storytelling can be a bulwark against a world in widespread decline, as it can be a point of genuine connection between strangers. You cannot stop the world from being mediocre, but you can write something that is fine and true and says exactly what you have to say. In Finishing School we put aside bravado and cheap cynicism and find satisfaction in making measurable progress toward this goal.

Doubt Parading as Pessimism: "I'll Never Get Published"

Cary

ANOTHER WAY WE try to avoid facing complicated and sometimes unpleasant emotions is to say, "I'll never get published." Like saying "I'm a terrible writer," saying "I'll never get published" accomplishes some things. We can feel powerful and in control. Unlike those other fools heedlessly throwing themselves into the hellish cauldron of risk and possibility, we can sit back, secure in the knowledge that we have seen the future! We know we will never get published, so why bother!

This is fine if you really don't want to be published.

But here is the catch: If you don't care, why are you even thinking about it? I never say to myself, "I know I'll never be a cop, so why bother applying to the academy?" I never say to myself, "I know I'll never be a postal functionary in Algeria, so why even go there and try to make the needed connections?"

On the other hand, I confess I have spent many hours calculating the odds of achieving this or that success in the field of writing, trying to manage my ambitions so they do not outstrip the likelihood of success. Maybe, I think to myself, if I'm lucky, I will go down in history as a midlevel author, an author of moderate success, a minor author with occasional flashes of real insight, a decent, respected American writer. Sometimes I allow myself to imagine being known as a writer of true ability, even genius. But then I see myself in the severe mirror of literary history and wonder if anyone heard me thinking such thoughts.

Why am I even thinking about this? Because for better or worse it matters to me. Okay? I admit it. It matters to me!

Could there be a more petty and ridiculous preoccupation? Is there no end to such silliness?

If you have this particular thought lodged in your brain, let me suggest a couple of things.

Of course, do Finishing School. By making regular weekly progress and checking in with others who are also making progress, you will start to feel more comfortable with the whole notion of trying to get published. It will feel a lot more real and normal.

You will probably continue to think from time to time, "I'll never get published!"

How to climb out of that primordial swamp of fears and wishes? Here are a couple of things you can do. One is to really, really, really face the fact that anything can happen. Contemplate surprise successes. Look at lottery winners. Look at overnight successes in publishing, in music. They happen. They are unexpected. No one predicts them. They just happen. No editor knows what book will be a hit. You can't know, either. So relax.

The other part is to face the downside. Contemplate true defeat. Examine your feelings about it. How bad will you feel if you try and try and do not get everything you hope to get? It is helpful to explore this. What would that actually mean?

You have to come up with your own answers, but I would suggest that one thing it would mean is that you could look at yourself in the mirror and say, "I tried! I gave it everything! I never second-guessed myself. I was true to my calling. And some things in this world are beyond any individual's control."

Social scientists have found that people are more likely to regret failing to try. It doesn't hurt so much if you tried and failed. It does not weigh so heavily on the conscience. But failure to try can really haunt you.

So try, at least.

If you actually do have a hunger to be published, then get to work! Get published somewhere. Anywhere. Now. You can get published somewhere. Start small. Build on little successes. Publish little things in small places. The satisfaction is out of all proportion to the venue—believe me. It's a kick!

And then you are a published writer. You don't have to publish a book to be a published writer.

"What about self-publishing?" you ask. Well, I think considering the amount of work that's involved in self-publishing a book, it's better to start by getting small pieces published in little papers and journals.

Not only is it easier, but you learn so much with every piece! You learn so much from editors and publishers. Even the smallest, most modest publication is still run by someone who, by dint of his or her involvement in the trade, knows a thing or two about writing. You can learn from these people. You can learn what kinds of things they like to publish, which means, incidentally, what kinds of things people like to read. You have a voice in the community then. People are reading your words. It's invaluable experience, and it's fun.

◗◆

Shame
"I Am Ashamed of
Not Finishing and Too
Ashamed to Finish"

Are You Lying to Yourself?

Danelle

You recognize the feeling when you see it on your friend's face. First hugs, chitchat. Then the question you've been wanting to ask since you last saw him six months ago: "How's the novel coming?" His smile pulls back, and the light in his eyes fades to a little flash of shame. "Great," he says disingenuously. "Coming right along."

I've done this too, but from the other side: that dinner party where I spin out the basic beats of my story or find myself quoting a passage from memory. The table is silent as the guests lean in to hear a juicy anecdote, the most well-developed part of the book so far. At the close of this oft-told tale, everyone is smiling. "I can't wait to read it," one says. "Let us know when it's done and we'll be sure to order it," says another. "We're so honored to have a real writer in our midst," says the host.

Even as those compliments wash over me, I feel like a fraud.

It's work to keep the smile on my face. The truth is that, just like my friend, I haven't touched my book in months. I've been dining out on that same section of the story for two years, and it's becoming harder and harder to remember why I decided I had an idea that was worthy of a book.

I had a story I'd tell at parties, about going to meet a serial killer because he was central to a work of nonfiction I was writing. The details of finding him on the Internet and journeying to prison to see him during visiting hours were so lurid and dramatic that every time I told the story my stature at the dinner party went up a few notches. Inside, I knew I was lying to myself. I'd done that one thing, and had an ongoing correspondence with the prisoner, but I hadn't touched the larger story in months. Cary used to read aloud excerpts from his novel that people found magical. They heaped him with praise. He didn't care to tell them that he'd written that passage ten years earlier. Both of us were losing credibility with the most important person in this whole endeavor: ourselves.

There are plenty of ways we lie to ourselves. We lie to ourselves about whether or not we are working and how much time we are spending on that work. We also lie to our loved ones, saying we have to go off and write but spending that time on something else. Although these are just little lies to avoid revealing the painful state of our writing, lying harms the work and harms the writer. The work of the writer is to tell the truth and to expose vulnerabilities in the human condition. If you are lying to yourself, it can seep into the work and result in cheap shortcuts and shoddy craft.

What we found through Finishing School is that if you meet weekly with others who are also trying to stay on track with a project, the lying stops. It's not necessary. You are working, therefore you have nothing to cover up. Defining the time and the structure through Finishing School, plus enjoying the camaraderie of other writers who are getting work done, means you can be honest at that party. "I'm struggling to finish my novel, but I'm determined to make it happen."

Discuss the ideas in this book with others, and we guarantee you will get nods of empathy and perhaps begin a conversation about other people's unfinished projects. You will find company rather than alienation. That is bound to fuel you on your path to finishing.

"Everyone Knows I'm a Failure": The Monologue That Stops You Cold

Danelle

WRITERS OFTEN FEEL puny when they compare themselves to the immensity of their dreams. This is where shame gets its hooks in. One definition of "shame" is that it arises when you compare your actions to your standards. This is the shame that stops writers from writing. They look at their writing lives and see only their feeble efforts, lack of discipline, and how befuddled they can be trying to figure out what they are trying to say, and they feel ashamed.

Inside us, shame feels different from guilt or regret. We might be able to argue ourselves out of a regret by citing the circumstances that surrounded it, or rationalize guilt as imposed on us by others, but shame is something we believe when it strikes. We can have a vague regret, but not a vague shame. We might feel regret wishing we had finished college, or guilt that we should have made a bigger fuss about our parents' twenty-fifth anniversary. These are wisps of feeling compared to what happens when shame takes over the body.

Shame pervades every cell. It is convincing. I may not believe my regrets, but I'm always certain about shame.

The shame monologue starts first in the body in the form of a cringe. The body involuntarily shrinks back, fearful that someone is about to strike it. Sometimes when I feel shame, I put my hands over my face to block out the world. One of the roots of the word "shame" is to cover, either to cover yourself in shame or to cover the parts of you that you are ashamed to show. I cover my face because I want to block out the shame and the eyes of the world that see my shame.

Once the shame monologue has begun, it must be recited all the way to the end, like a mantra of humiliation. It is a bodily manifestation of many of the insecurities that support the emotional pitfalls: "Everyone knows I'm a failure. There is nothing unique about me. I've got nothing new to say. Look at that miserable sentence. It is arrogant of me to think anyone would want to read that, or anything else I've written. I'm terrified that someone will read this and think I am as mediocre as the things I write. Every time they ask me about my novel, they secretly know I'll never finish. They're just waiting for me to give up and admit I failed."

Shame runs deep, and it has a way of persuading us that it is pointless to finish our work. Hours pass. Pages go unwritten. The shame monologue doesn't help to alleviate the condition. Instead, it is a confirmation of all we fear about our unworthiness.

The longer you neglect your writing, the more ashamed of it you become. Without consistent engagement, the doubts rush in, and when you think of it, you don't think of it as having problems you can solve but as being so flawed and unoriginal that to go back to it means having to face its weaknesses, which shame has merged with your own. Thinking about your writing, you cringe. That's a tough place from which to write.

This makes the battle with shame one of the hardest fought of all the emotional pitfalls. The battle is interior, and exterior too.

Getting rid of this "everyone knows" thought is the first battlefront against shame. The truth is that "everyone" is not paying much attention to your dreams. Most people are so absorbed in their own shortcomings that they don't have much space left over to consider yours. And, anyway, most of them have not read your writing. The truth is that you are just imagining they are judging you. The rest of the world does not think you are a failure; it's you. And you are so ashamed. Yet in some way it is easier to imagine that the shame comes from something others are saying about you, rather than accepting that it is something of your creation. The imagined idea that others are making you feel ashamed is easier to shake off than the self-generated assurance of your mediocrity.

Either way, whether imagined as something visited on you by a brutal world or created from your imagined lack of value, shame has to be confronted, even if it cannot be solved. The only way to battle shame is by continuing to work.

You cannot control the amount of self-loathing you generate, but you can control how much time and effort you put into your work. Being consistent at writing is the defense against shame. We all come to the task of writing with different levels of skill and different amounts of time. Completing a piece of writing will take longer for some than for others. If you keep at it, you will finish. You have not failed if you are still trying. If you are still writing, you are still in the fight.

This fight is different from the fight against the other emotional pitfalls, some of which can be dismissed by an insight or a rationale. Not shame.

When we were outlining this book, sitting around a kitchen table in the Berkeley Hills, I said, "We really aren't writing enough about shame."

There was a pause then, during which we let that feeling of shame, always close by, move up through our bodies. Cary nodded his head yes, in agreement, then said aloud as he jotted in his assignment notebook, "Note to self: look into the bottomless pit of despair and report back."

Indeed, who signs up for the gruesome task of revealing our weakest acts and probing our lapses in character? Writers. Writing brings with it a considerable tussle with shame. When you are writing, often you are looking at times in your life when you felt ashamed. That is where some of the best writing may be: in describing those conditions and decisions, as well as the people who shamed you.

This creates an additional complication: your writing may be asking you to reveal things, from your life and the lives of others, that are shameful. The resistance to admitting these actions, and to exploring them, to taking the blame for the difference between your standards and your actions, is another powerful barrier to work.

In Cary's Amherst Writers and Artists writing workshops, he sometimes does an exercise about shame, called "Taboo." Students write about taboo subjects, the actions that make us cringe, like eating feces, incest, gambling away a child's college fund, or betraying the trust of a dear friend. The room is full of tension as the exercise begins, because writing about these topics is uncomfortable. The guilt and disgust that taboos generate freeze the students in place at first. They ask themselves tough questions. How could I do that? What could make my character take such an action? Answering those questions well can generate some interesting writing and, Cary says, the exercise is liberating. By the end of the writing time, the room is full of energy and laughter. Those who have faced this shame are liberated from it, released from the hold it has on their writing. Writing about shame and feeling it move through the body can lessen its grip. In this way writing can be an antidote to shame.

When you make measurable progress week after week in Finishing School, you realize that because you are on a path to success, you are less likely to be seen as a failure. You also realize that you don't have to hide what you are doing, because what you are doing is leading you toward a laudable and attainable goal. You can stop lying. As you present yourself with empirical evidence of your progress, your self-esteem grows. Your inner monologue is eventually no match for the obvious fact that you are succeeding.

"I'm Letting the World Down by Not Being a Total Genius": The Problem with Early Potential

Cary

"You HAVE so much potential." Even today, my gut wrenches at the words.

Has anyone ever told you that you have great potential? Who told you this? Was it a teacher? Was it a coach? What did they mean when they said you had great potential?

I was told I had potential. I was told in a scientific way. I was studied with the latest instruments. Scientists peered inside me and saw the potential I could not see.

Actually, my father told me many times that I had great potential. He was that scientist. My case is unusual in that my father actually measured my potential. He was ideally suited to do so, being an educational psychologist who specialized in testing and measurement. So he tested and measured my potential.

What did being told I had great potential do for me? Did it

help? Did it fill me with confidence about a bright and exciting future? No. Actually, it gave me the notion that I could probably fail with impunity and catch up later. It also angered me. It did not feel like praise but like a vague threat: it made me feel as though this thing I had belonged to others, as though I were a natural resource to be mined, as though it were my job to harness this potential for the good of others.

True, I initially felt a swelling of satisfaction about my prospects. I knew I was smart. But I also felt resentful. That resentment was compounded when any lack of success was met with the frowning, worried imprecation "But you have such potential!"

Why did I feel angry at my father and mother and teachers for telling me I had potential? I felt they were claiming ownership of something that was mine. If I had this potential, then it was mine. It was *my* potential, to do with as I saw fit. It was the ability for me to meet my own needs.

But not according to the adults. They were more concerned with this potential than they were with me, the actual person in whom it resided. So I rebelled. If I had potential, why bother with schoolwork? Why bother with small tasks? I could always catch up when I felt like it.

I became an angry underachiever. I went on a sort of achievement strike. I failed. I deliberately failed. But out of this failure came feelings of guilt and shame.

I had been the smart kid, the good kid, the golden boy. I was the one in whom educators took a special interest. If I was so full of potential and not developing it, then I must be a bad person. If the right thing to do was to develop your potential to its highest, then I must be selfish and unworthy of respect.

Rather than a cheerful young man gradually acquiring life skills and understanding, I became an angry, spiteful, and guilt-ridden student.

Maybe that sounds pretty awful. But I want to try to reach the hearts of others who feel the same way and have not worked it out yet for themselves. By speaking with this voice that is still pained and awkward, that has not figured it all out yet and made peace with it, I may strike a chord with others who still carry this burden of being the chosen one, the favorite, the gifted child. And, yes, I have read Alice Miller's book *The Drama of the Gifted Child*, and revisiting these feelings reminds me that I could stand to read it again.

This is really what the problem of early potential is all about: the conflict that arises from presenting a false self to meet emotional needs. It isn't really so much about the problem of early potential per se. It's what the child does with that early potential. It's how we allow ourselves to be twisted and distorted in our true being by the ways in which we have met and still meet the needs of adults.

In later life, living with unrealizable potential brings anxiety and weariness. We become weary because we cannot stop searching for this thing. We cannot stop searching for it because we cannot know if we have ever found it. It is illusory and intangible. It *is potential.*

So we may carry on in a state of low-level anxiety and a sense that we will never feel fulfilled. Or we may attempt to discharge this haunting potential in a fantastic explosion of excess. That is another way to rid ourselves of this burdensome potential: to commit arson upon ourselves. We try to burn it all up. We write heedlessly until we drop; we paint without ceasing; we attempt to become the best ever at something by devoting every hour to it because any hour not devoted to it is an hour spent in the agony of unfulfilled potential. This is how some of us creative types respond to the inexhaustible and debilitating challenge of being told we have potential: we burn it up.

The problem with potential is that you can never reach it. Having been told you have potential opens up a vast gulf between you and whatever that potential might represent. It opens up a vast gulf between who you are and who you might be. That person you *might be* then haunts you and taunts you.

Being the child with great potential also harms your later prospects in this way: If you can skate by, you don't learn to work hard. If you can always come up with something passable at the last minute, you don't learn to struggle and persist and think things through and solve difficult problems. You don't develop those skills, that craft, those habits that less precocious young people learn.

If there is a pedagogical point to this last observation, it may be this: *emotion fuels creative work*. All this emotion that is so exhausting to confront and feel and write from—this is the *energy source* of creative work. But it is also, paradoxically, the soul-threatening knowledge of need and vulnerability, and thus the very thing that, unconsciously, threatens to take me down. (That's interesting, isn't it, the phrase "take me down"? For *down* is exactly the point; *down* is the emotional center from which the false self fled in its acting career, rather than face the potentially shameful, annihilating truth.)

I would like to follow my true, deep, intuitive path as an artist, but the things I would make will not necessarily give me the reassurance and support I crave. I am an extrovert, and I want to be known in the world as a creative artist, and that means I care, perhaps too much, about how my work is received. And because I identify so strongly with my work, I feel ashamed if it is not well received. I let judgments about the work become judgments about myself.

HERE IS HOW Finishing School can help. What I truly crave is not necessarily critical understanding and praise but simply acknowledgment that I am working. The way Finishing School works is that we are acknowledged just for showing up. It's very adult that way. We are not into each other's work. We recognize that each person is following a separate path and responsible for solving the aesthetic and practical problems that arise in their pursuit of their work. We're not here to solve anybody else's aesthetic problems. We are just here to say, "Great! You're doing your work! Keep going!" And, as it turns out, that's pretty much all we need.

And we find an answer to that nasty, vexing question that haunts those of us with potential: "Is that the best you can do?" To this we answer yes—in spite of whatever great potential you may believe we have, in spite of all the greatness that may be locked up inside of us, in spite of everything others have hoped and dreamed for us. Right here, right now, in this world, today, "This is the best I can do. Deal with it."

This encompasses not just our vaunted potential but also our emotions and our needs. It is to say, "I may harbor this potential you speak of, but I am also a human being with limits. No matter what you may think, I do not have limitless time or energy or intelligence. I am just a person. I am not a machine to be run until it shudders and flies apart; nor am I a quarry to be mined. I am not a resource. I am seeking my destiny and satisfaction in life just as you are." Our relationship, therefore, is not one of exploiter and resource. It is one human to another.

We are spirited and feeling humans. We do not seek to be exploited. We seek fulfillment and balance. We have some choice in what we will do. We are not driven to "fulfill our potential" in every human encounter. Any potential we have is, frankly, no one else's business. What is crucial is this: to ask ourselves, *what do we have to offer?* Now that this debilitating notion of potential is put to rest, what, in concrete terms, do we have to offer?

That is where Finishing School comes in. By committing to a method with clear, achievable goals, we can offer to others not some vague notion of our possible genius, but an actual work product. We can know precisely what we can and cannot produce, and we can negotiate on this basis. It is no longer a problem of promising an editor a piece and then going crazy, praying to the gods for inspiration. We know if we work a certain number of hours, in a controlled and planned way, at the end we will achieve an acceptable product. Moreover, this product need not be the proof of our long-vaunted potential, nor a measure of our worth as human beings. It is simply something to be traded for something else. It is, to be quite crass, a product. Of course, in producing it we may have had an aesthetic high; we may have acquired knowledge or hit upon the occasional ingenious solution or felicitous phrase. But the process has been one of clear, measured craft. It has not been an anxious battle to prove the prognostications of social scientists and educational psychologists about our so-called potential.

Setting clear goals also frees us of vulnerability to manipulation. If those who would manipulate and cheat us sense that what we really crave is not fair treatment but praise, not encouragement but flattery, then we may be persuaded to take less than our work is worth. We may be paid partly in ego stroking. When we are hollow with the emptiness of potential, we will seek anything that seems to fill us.

And it is a hollowness. That is the legacy of being told we have potential: we have been given the gift of emptiness. For that is what potential is in the end: a kind of emptiness into which we forever pour ourselves. Those of us with potential may never completely overcome our feelings of shame about it, but we can recognize how to use those feelings to drive toward solid, productive work.

Yearning
"Does My Dream of
Being a Writer Get in
the Way of My Writing?"

The Yearning for Perfection: "I Must Write the Perfect First Sentence or Else!"

Danelle

A FRIEND OF mine has been working on his novel for three months but cannot get past the first sentence. He says it has to be perfect. He has swapped out verbs, changed voices, tried different narrators. These are the first words the reader will read, he reminds me, so that sentence has to hint at something but not reveal too much, and do so in a way that establishes the voice of his novel. If the sentence lacks style or rhythm, he fears his reader may not go any further, and if he can't get the first sentence right, he doesn't see any point in going on. The requirements of that sentence have him confused and fearful, not sure what to write, so comma in, comma out, comma back again. In his fixation with this one sentence, you can see how the yearning for perfection can be a trap.

The yearning for perfection represents a truehearted goal that every writer aspires to meet. It motivates you to work long hours, really stretch yourself, trying to create a world where no detail is amiss. You owe your readers that. Perfection*ism* is something different: less of an aspiration and more of a conviction—a sentence that bangs around a dim space in the brain, like a pebble in a gourd.

Some things can be perfect. We can make a perfect square or a perfect circle because in the case of those geometric shapes perfection has precise and measurable tolerances. If you wish to make squares and circles, you can make something that is objectively perfect. This is perfection that comes from perfect control. In writing, as in other creative acts, perfection starts as imperfection. The perfect may be a true expression made by an unsteady hand. To create, you must be free.

I struggled with perfectionism when I was hired to help a renowned spiritual figure write a book about love. My job was to find the real-life stories she would use to illustrate her points. I saw myself as working in the basement of the book, fashioning her raw material. Many people had volunteered their love stories, and I would wake up every morning with my first thoughts being about love, eager to interview the people who had written to her and help them tell their stories.

I was also free to draw on my life for examples, and in thinking about love daily I grew to recognize love in places where I had not detected it before, which was the point of the book. I could think of stories that illustrated the way I loved my children, my family, my friends, and how I loved life itself. It made me happy to realize how many stories I had. Although I didn't have much trouble writing others' love stories, when I tried to write mine, perfectionism created a mania that stopped me.

Instead of waking up happy to have the chance to explore what I truly felt, I would think what I truly felt was second rate, cliché. Spiritual books connect to their readers through the common experience, but before I had my first cup of coffee, I was convinced that my experience was too common to be worth much to anyone. I had big words like "truth" and "passion" and "honesty" hanging around my head in a cloud, which inhibited me from writing a basic factual sentence like "John walked into the bedroom." I was honored to have this job helping someone I respected, but, to be satisfied, what I wrote for her needed not to just be true, but even truer than true. True on a multitude of levels, true for the ages and for all beings. It was as if I were ghostwriting for God, yet unable to present my flawed self to the all-forgiving deity because I was unworthy. The grip of this on my mind was so tight that I did not see the irony in it. Many times I sat in that emptiness in a panic of doubt, yet I think this was the year of my greatest growth as a writer.

Eventually I identified the contrast between the ease with which I wrote others' stories and the agony I felt writing mine. My heart understood other people's revelations about loss or acts of generosity without needing too many details. If they stumbled or acted poorly, I identified with them more strongly. When I spoke with them about their stories, those moments were the places in the narrative where I wanted to know more. In my writing about me, I didn't want just to write a perfect story; I wanted to *be* perfect. Clearly I had not absorbed the book's lessons on love for the self. In overidentifying with perfection, I saw only my inadequacies and I could not write at all.

The yearning for perfection burdened my writing with expectations that made me unable to be free and creative. What

I was trying to write was perfect in my conception of it, but when that perfection came up against my insecurities, the beautiful vision evaporated. The cacophony of perfectionism, all the voices of judgment, left me unable to hear what I had to say.

In decades as a journalist, I've listened to thousands of voices: the mannered voices of powerful people and self-important celebrities and ordinary people confronted by extraordinary circumstances. My position as their audience is to maintain for them a safe space where they are free to say what they think in the words that come naturally to them. They may talk for hours, going down side roads and making incoherent declarations, while I focus completely on trying to sift out the truth from all those words. I hear them in a way they never have been heard before.

Most times when I start working with someone, I transcribe the first interview myself, to get a sense of how they phrase things. If the person stumbles over words or uses wrong ones, or has grammatical quirks in the way he or she speaks, I am alert to these traits as perfect expressions of who they are. Not perfect like an opera singer's aria, but perfect because they are unique to that person, who struggles to say something in the way only they can say it.

In writing we are trying to do with ourselves what I am doing for the people I work with, to hear ourselves rather than the voices of the judges and critics. To get around the trap of perfectionism, I learned, I had to open the space around me as I did for the people I interviewed. Yearning for perfection can stop you from hearing that authentic voice, which says inconsistent things. And while others might not see perfection in such a voice, when you teach yourself how to listen you see that it is perfect in a way of its own.

What I wanted to advise my friend was to stop trying to make that first sentence perfect. To give up the quest for perfection completely for a time, so he could restore the joy behind telling his story. As Julia Cameron wrote in *Finding Water: The Art of Perseverance*: "Perfectionism doesn't believe in practice shots. It doesn't believe in improvement. . . . The critic does not believe in creative glee—or any glee at all, for that matter. No, perfectionism is a serious matter." Yes, writing is a serious matter, but it is one that begins in play, not in the vice grip I had endured and that my friend was living through with that sentence.

In reality, my friend is not equipped to write that first sentence because he hasn't yet written enough of the novel. What he considers a perfect first sentence today could be completely different when he has 150 pages written and the characters have changed, and he's decided to set the story in Texas instead of in Mendocino. As Joyce Carol Oates said in a 1986 interview with *Writer's Digest*, "The first sentence can't be written until the final sentence is written." Perfection is not for the first sentence, nor for the first draft. It may be for the second draft or the tenth, but in all of this, at every step, the goal is to feel free.

The Trap of Symbolic Victories: Resisting the Clarion Call of the Office Supply Store

Cary

MAYBE SOMETHING LIKE this has happened to you. Say you are ready to get to work on your project, and you are in your workspace. Then you realize you need some file folders, because stacked about you are piles of paper: notes, research, draft chapters, an outline, correspondence. You can't find what you need quickly and easily, and this makes you angry and frustrated. So you think, "Actually, instead of what I had planned, a great way to spend this time would be to go to the office supply store!"

Off you go to Staples, feeling this is the best use of your time because finally you are going to get those files in order. You come home with an armful of brightly colored file folders, and you rip the plastic off them and put them on your desk next to the stacks of disordered notes and chapters. Then you realize that the time you allotted to work on your project is nearly up. You have not moved the writing forward at all.

This is what Danelle and I call the "trap of symbolic victory": instead of making tangible progress in our work, we substitute some symbolic act or acquisition. It makes us feel good, but it doesn't move the project forward. It feels like victory, but it is really a form of slow, insidious defeat.

People who are creative must take advantage of inspiration, so we are allowed to change our plans. But there is inspiration, and there is running off to the office supply store.

In Finishing School we think it is better, in a moment of frustration or discomfort, to stop for a moment, admit that you are feeling frustrated, and take a breath. Then e-mail or text your creative buddy—another Finishing School class member with whom you check in each time you sit down to work and when you finish that session—and say, "Hey, I'm feeling frustrated. I'm in danger of going to Staples for office supplies."

In Finishing School you can do that. The minute you notice that you are even thinking about deviating from what you set out to do, you can text or e-mail your creative buddy.

Let's take a minute to really think about this. You say you are going to do one thing, and then you do something else. You make an appointment, and then you blow it off. If you were meeting your creative buddy for coffee and decided to go look at a nice office chair instead, your creative buddy would be upset. Think about avoiding your scheduled writing time in the same way. You are not showing up for your appointment. Maybe nobody is standing on a street corner waiting for you. Just the same, you have an appointment and you're not showing up for it. You might even say that it's your creative destiny standing on that street corner, waiting for you to show up, wondering why you changed your mind.

Let's go deeper. What happens psychologically, or emotionally, when we do something like that? It is like we are abandoning our own spirit, the godlike part of ourselves, the sacred in us. What powerful force is it that drives us to run from our own spirit, our own calling? It must be something!

Let's focus on this moment, right now, when you are reading these words and thinking about changing your life. You are reading this because you have certain dreams and want certain things. You want to bring certain things into being. You want to find out if you can do those things. You want to make them happen.

Time is limited. I am a cancer survivor and I know that time is limited. When I pretend that it's no big deal, when I figure I'll get to it later, when I go to the office supply store thinking, "I'll do the writing tomorrow," here is how I feel: I feel like I'm slipping. I feel like I'm wasting my life.

There are certain things I want and need to make me happy, and certain things I can live without.

I can live without the file folders.

What I really need is to fulfill my creative destiny. If it were an actual, conscious choice between fulfilling my creative destiny and having some new file folders, I know what choice I would make. So how does it happen that I get up from my chair and go to the car and drive to Staples—as I have done more than once? I'm like a man who is sleepwalking.

What I really want to be doing is writing. Writing means sitting in the chair. Anything that helps me sit in the chair is something I want to hold on to. Anything that gets in the way is something I want to avoid.

It's important to remember that this seemingly inexplicable decision to get up from the writing desk and go to Staples does not happen in a vacuum. It happens in a culture of phenomenal distraction. Our culture is full of lures and snares designed to get me out of that chair and into a store to buy something. To do our creative work, we have to actively resist this powerful, masterful, ingenious arrangement of lures and enticements.

In that sense, the techniques of Finishing School are tools of cultural defiance. Finishing School is our quiet, orderly defiance of all the lures and tricks of marketing.

This is not a game for me, and I do not think it is a game for you. There is real spiritual suffering in substituting a false, symbolic item for the real thing. So when you are sitting there trying to write and it seems like a good idea to go buy some file folders, think about what's really going on in that moment.

Think about the rest of your life.

OF COURSE, THE problem is exactly this: The powerful emotions that drive us to get up from the chair and go to Staples to buy file folders actually cloud our thinking. At the very moment when we need to think clearly and ask ourselves, "Do I want to go to the office supply store, or do I want to save my soul?" our heads are muddled by some emotion, and it is as if we say to ourselves, "Fuck saving my soul! I'm going to Staples for purple file folders."

I know this: In that moment, I do not know what has come

over me. I find myself surfing the Internet or thinking about ice cream because what has happened, actually, is that I have had some powerful emotion whose source is yet unclear, and I want to run away from it.

I used to respond in such moments of unease by having a drink, which would usually ruin the writing for the day, because it would never be just one drink. Now, of course, other substitute distractions present themselves, but I have to learn to sit here and ask, what is going on? Am I thinking about my father again, feeling guilty for not having been able to help him more? Am I feeling angry toward him for not giving me the tools for living that I so craved and needed? Am I feeling sad and desperate because I am sixty-two years old and have not yet published the big novel? Am I just feeling lonely and wishing I were shooting basketball hoops with my older brother, David, wishing I were sixteen again?

I could go on forever having such thoughts. It's tempting to write a whole different chapter, based on the ideas and feelings that flood my mind when I think about being distracted. These are real emotions that come over me when I am trying to write something. They won't just go away. I have to deal with them. One way to deal with them is to ask, okay, what have these emotions to do with what I am currently writing? How can they be of service to me? They can be of service to me by reminding me that my life is real and precious and there is no turning back now. There is no pretending. I sit back in my chair. I take a sip of green tea. I keep sitting here. If I am going to quit, I need to e-mail my creative buddy first and say I am quitting. I am not going to quit. I am going to keep going. My eyes are tired. I remove my glasses and rub my eyes. I focus on something in the distance. The valley stretches out before me. It is only 10:48 a.m. I have until 2:30 p.m. I slump back in my chair and put my hands on the arms and blow out a big breath, puffing out my cheeks. I stare at the screen.

There is nothing for me to do but sit in this chair and think of Alberto Giacometti, the great Swiss sculptor and painter who faced the seemingly impossible task of completing a work of art with a grimly cheerful blend of fatalism and obstinacy: "The more you fail, the more you succeed. It is only when everything is lost and—instead of giving up—you go on, that you experience the momentary prospect of some slight progress. Suddenly you have the feeling—be it an illusion or not—that something new has opened up."

For it is an impossible task. We admit it. What we are doing is impossible. Yet there is no other way to persist in life with any dignity except by continuing to do this thing. If I abandon this thing, then all life feels hopeless. If I allow myself to be distracted, I am just an idiot, a child, not a man, a grown-up. If I am distracted by shiny things that sing banal electronic melodies when I am trying to save my soul by doing the one thing I know how to do that brings purpose and meaning to my life, then I am a child, a puppet, a hopeless case. If I allow myself to be distracted this morning, tomorrow will be worse. I will be further from my goal. I must push on.

So I get up and walk around my chair. I have a snack. That is permitted. I have a glass of water. I return to the chair.

I look at the time. Nine minutes have passed. It is 10:57 in the morning. I have until 2:30. I am exhausted. This is serious. This is how I must behave. This is the rigor, and the crazy, deep, sad, desperate state I must be in if I am to persist.

This sort of thing can go on for a long time. If I hadn't set aside the time that I am planning to work, and if I hadn't told someone else about it, and hadn't committed to doing it, I could walk away. I could give into the distraction and the frustration and the sense of difficulty and uncertainty that is my frequent companion when I am trying to write. But I don't do that, because I don't have to, and neither do you.

That is why I am sharing this with you. I am trying to help you by sharing this with you. You don't have to respond to the discomfort or the voices or the lure of illusory satisfactions to be had outside your little room where you are writing. That is why I am doing this. I am showing the way. This is how you do it. Let nothing stand in your way.

Now I have written these things and immediately I am afraid. I want to go back and fix everything, make sure it is all smooth, make sure I have said nothing embarrassing or egotistical. I keep going. There is another chapter to work on.

ANOTHER KIND OF symbolic victory is even worse. At least in the first instance we are writing but being distracted. This other kind of symbolic victory keeps us from even getting started. It is the belief that one must have the proper things before one begins. This delusion is aided by our culture of acquisition and celebrity, a culture whose members worship the accoutrements of success more than the achievement that brought that success. Say you are thinking of writing something and so you quite sensibly begin to look at other writers and how they have done it. You may find yourself seduced by pictures of writers at work. I have been. There are certain writer-at-work pictures I find so charming and seductive that they can literally stop me from writing. But at least I am already writing and I know that it is not a very glamorous thing while you are doing it. But say you have been utterly taken by certain images of writers at work, and you look at the shirt, the bedstead, the desk, the window, and you think, that is how I will get this book done: I will get a desk like that at a window like that and I will wear a shirt like that and that's how I will get the book done.

So you get the desk and the window and the shirt and the chair and you dismiss the decorators and sit in the chair. Now what? You're in the same situation I am in. You're just sitting in a chair. You may like the desk and the window and the shirt, but you are still just a writer in a chair. It's wonderful in a way because it means you have joined the great society of people drawn to write, and you are feeling what everyone else feels. Your chair may be better than mine, and you may have a really nice pen, but otherwise we are on a level playing field, because everything that happens now happens within you; each of us is solitary. In a noisy Brooklyn loft or in a farmhouse in Vermont or in a bungalow in Palo Alto or in an apartment overlooking the square in a small Tuscan town—it doesn't matter. What matters is what goes on inside you once you are sitting there. Can you stay there in that lovely chair, writing at the lovely desk, looking out that lovely window long enough to find your subject and be true to it? Isn't that what you are truly yearning for? That is all that matters. That is the only thing between you and whatever success you imagine. You have to just stay in the chair.

The Yearning for Acclaim:
The Sore Loser Award

Danelle

THERE ARE MOMENTS when you write something that is excellent and you know it. Even if you've been writing for decades, hundreds of thousands of words, or you have just begun as a writer and have crafted a small gem of a poem, you feel this resonance with the words you've written. Of course you want someone to notice, and it's even better if they certify you as the best.

As you sit at the desk, dreading how hard it is to get published, the mind leaps over the potential risks and humiliations and lands directly in a life of international celebrity. The wish that someone would pay attention quickly moves from a modest hope to a yearning for acclaim.

In my fantasy where I accept the National Book Award, I'm gracious and generous, witty and well dressed. I'm also a decade younger, many pounds lighter, and wearing really expensive lingerie. I've got two versions of this little movie actually: one in which I know almost everyone at the award luncheon, because those who judge the contest are friends of mine, many of whom are talking about how this really is my year; and another one in which I'm unknown, distant, ironic, subversive, and dressed in black. This latter version of me believes awards are a pointless spectacle of elite self-congratulation and is attending only because, sure I'm not going to win, I want to mock those who take this seriously. When I win unexpectedly, my acceptance speech is subtly ironic; only a scattered few in the crowd are quick enough to get my jokes.

Those two fantasies played in regular rotation for decades until 2010, when a story I wrote for *San Francisco* magazine was a finalist for the National Magazine Award. I found out then what a sore loser I am. I know it is an honor to be nominated, but if I'm not going to win, please leave me alone.

I'd spent a year and a half working on the story of one rapacious family's early manipulations of the city's overheated real estate market. The story was close to my heart because I am a San Francisco native and in writing it I was able to describe the city as I saw and loved it, and how that city was disappearing. I was joyful when I received word I had made the cut. I burned up the phone lines telling dozens of people about this honor—Facebook and all the rest. When I read the other nominees' stories, I decided I had a better than even chance to win this thing.

After that brief moment of satisfaction came a six-week state of emergency.

It had been a rough few years for me financially, after the 2008 economic downturn when fees for writing books and articles dropped dramatically. As an associate bureau chief at *People* magazine's Los Angeles bureau, I had had a pretty nice wardrobe, but things had gone downhill in that department since I started working from home. I'd gained a lot of weight and I was going to be in a room with many people I hadn't seen in years. I had to buy a new outfit and was even more alarmed when I discovered that the clothes that fit me best were in the plus-size department. As I crammed myself into one of these unfashionable outfits, vowing to lose twenty pounds before the ceremony, I was terrified by what my former colleagues would think when they saw me. They were going to take one look at me on that evening, the zenith of my career so far, and think, "What the hell happened to her?" When I won and I hauled my big fat ass up to the podium, viewers all over the world would be asking themselves the same question.

I got over that, or rather I plunged forward anyway. The magazine put me up in an elegant boutique hotel on West Forty-Sixth Street and Eighth Avenue. I'd made an appointment to get my hair done at a salon a few blocks away the afternoon before the award ceremony. Everybody at the salon made a big fuss over me when the staff found out I was a finalist. They really saw me coming. I was shocked when I saw that the bill for fluffing up my self-esteem came to $250, but I didn't want to break up that feeling of graciously sliding into victory by objecting, so onto the credit card it went.

As I strolled down Eighth Avenue back to the hotel to get dressed, it occurred to me that I needed to have an acceptance speech ready. I wasn't sure what to say. I ducked into a Starbucks and sat at the window with my pencil poised over my notebook, looking at all the people walking down Eighth Avenue: the preppy Wall Street guy in Brooks Brothers, a fashion model carrying a portfolio that seemed to weigh as much as she did, a clutch of tourists who had stopped in the middle of the sidewalk to stare, a mom and her toddler, and a guy pushing a huge rack of clothing. How can we tell stories, I wondered, that could reach all these different kinds of people, all these backgrounds and ethnicities? That was our duty, no matter what format the stories came in. Storytelling was the thing everyone in the audience that night did well, and it was something that could bring all these different kinds of people together. My heart was full as I started to write my remarks. When I got back to the hotel, I called a friend in California and read them to her, and she had a catch in her voice when she assured me that these words were the ones that would be remembered.

The tickets to this shindig were five hundred dollars each, and every magazine in New York had sent a few people. Hundreds of us jammed into the lobby of Alice Tully Hall, a big concert venue on Manhattan's Upper West Side, where drinks and appetizers were abundant. I saw many old friends, and each time I saw them react with surprise at how I looked it reinforced my self-consciousness. During the cocktail hour, I found out that because this was the American Society of Magazine Editors, my *editor* would be accepting the award, not me, so I would not be speaking.

I sat, impatient that they call my category so I could release this anxiety. I thought I would explode with joy, but instead I collapsed inward when they announced that Atul Gawande of the *New Yorker* had won in the public-interest category. The whole room was applauding, but not me. Atul Gawande. No, Atul FUCKING Gawande, the Harvard graduate, the top surgeon at Brigham and Women's Hospital, the *New Yorker* staffer and best-selling author, just won again. Why does Atul Gawande

get to have it all? He had so many awards, he couldn't be both-
ered to be here to collect this one. He was busy up in Boston,
saving lives, that asshole. I was left to take my misshapen fantasies, noble sentiments, and overpriced haircut back to my hovel
in California.

Both of the fantasies that had filled my imagination were
absurdly inaccurate. In either scenario someone besides me
was the protagonist, some cartoon of world domination inspired by feelings of unworthiness. I was not the insider and,
in truth, would never be. When I was standing at the top of the
stairs, looking down at the people who run the magazine
world, I was frightened to be among them. There were editors
there but also the corporate publishers, the investors, repre-
sentatives from the big ad agencies, all the members of the
club. Yet I could not be an ironic outsider either, because I
cared too much. I was the woman who sat at the window,
thinking about all the people a well-told story could reach and
how hard it was to do that.

THIS IS THE dark side of yearning that has little to do with
story and truth. Many fine writers spend whole careers never
earning recognition and, instead of inspiring them to write
more and better, these elaborate fantasies stir up bitterness
and make them feel like failures.

Recognize that dreams of fame and stardom can leave us
helpless and out of touch with reality. Don't fall for the con. Do
not burden your writing with impossible expectations.

Fear
"What Am I Actually Afraid Of?"

"Who the Hell Am I to Think I Can Write?"

Danelle

AT A DINNER party I was talking to another guest about my work as a collaborator on book projects. I shared with her the happy news that I recently had been hired to work on a book with a well-known thinker who was held in high esteem by many people, including the woman to whom I was speaking. When she found out whom I was working with, the woman asked, "What qualifies you to work on this book?"

This question straightened my back. The first thing I thought to say was, "What qualifies you to ask that question?" Quickly after that, I found myself agreeing with her underlying doubts. Indeed, there was nothing, as far as I could see, that qualified me, except that I knew something about the subject and I was a good partner in any project. But I did not say that. Instead, I responded: "The fact that I was hired."

The day after the party I couldn't get that woman's question out of my head. All alone in my apartment, thinking about the big questions presented by this book, every time my mind started to take flight, I was stopped by those words from a stranger. Used to working quickly, I had to slow down. I wasn't writing, but I couldn't leave the apartment. Lying on the couch, staring at the ceiling, looking out the window. Watching a lot of *Law & Order*, which seems to be always running on some channel somewhere. Every time I walked out into the street, I squinted at the sunlight. When asked the question, who am I to write? I did not have a very good answer. A simple statement from a stranger disrupted the confidence I'd built after decades as a writer and made me question whether I was worthy of the job my coauthor had chosen me to do. She thought I was worthy of the task, but after one question, I was not so sure.

It is so simple a question that, once you consider it legitimate, it seems to call everything about life into doubt.

Who the hell am I to think that anyone wants to hear what I have to say? Writers wrestle with this doubt often when they look at their work or think about the fact that they are not working and dread returning. The sentences that don't look good on the page, or don't sound right, and the paragraphs that say something other than what you wanted to say, or not enough of it, these, instead of the emotions and ideas that drove you to write, make you feel incompetent or stupid, unworthy of the task. This is particularly so if you have in mind a cherished author whose work you strive to emulate.

You must fight this. Filling your mind with these doubts about your value in the world leaves no space for writing. You cannot write with a brain filled with self-abuse. The answers to, who the hell am I? rise like vapor from this swamp. I am a loser, a failure, a fraud. I am an idiot to think I could ever be a writer. I don't have the skill or the drive or the time, and, besides, what I have to say sounds like everyone else. I'm a nobody and no one will ever listen to me.

The writer fights this feeling by continuing to work. By writing, you are fighting for the right to have something to say, and saying it even if no one wants to listen. You have been gifted with a defined point of view. You see the world in a way that others do not. Something happened to you that shaped these traits and drove you to try to communicate them, if only to make you understand yourself better. The way you put things together has a meaning that is indistinct to others. Expressing this clearly is not easy. This does not mean the task is impossible or that you are not worthy. It means it's tough for anyone who takes it seriously.

But more than that, you have to fight against all the people who will tell you that you have nothing to say and could never be a writer. Against everyone who snorted at one of your ideas and all the people who didn't get your jokes and made you feel bad because of it. For every time you pointed out something that was going on and were ignored. Fight against the people who refused to listen. All the people who told you that your story was just like everyone else's, so why should it matter? The real question is: who the hell are they?

Who the hell are they to judge your value in such an offhand way? Who the hell are they to say that you can't do it and shouldn't try? The truth is most of them are barely paying attention to their own lives, to the people they are around, and to the responsibilities they are supposed to fulfill. You write to wake yourself to those around you, because you can see that the majority of people are fully or partially asleep. Yet when you muster the courage to share with them your heartfelt desire to write, they do not call you brave or noble or wish you well. They roll their eyes at your dream.

The answer to the question is to write. You write primarily for yourself, and your objective is to say something as clearly and strongly as you can, no matter how long it takes. But also sometimes you write with a chip on your shoulder, to prove those people wrong. Everyone who puffed out a blast of contempt at your pledge to write, the people who were cruel in response and set you back weeks or months with a single comment. But most of all you write to prove it to yourself, the observer who is the meanest of the bunch. You've taken every slight and rejection to heart and magnified them many times over. They are the reason you ask yourself this question. You're the primary proponent of the idea that you don't deserve to be a writer.

The problem with calling yourself a writer is all you attach to that word. You may want to write like one of your favorite authors, so you think you will become a writer when you write like that person. Or perhaps you think the writer's state will be achieved when you are published or you make money or become self-supporting. Maybe nothing less than a best seller will satisfy you. Whatever way you define it, likely you're not measuring up to that definition.

Being a writer is not a finished state but an ongoing practice. It is a struggle that many abandon. Who the hell are you? You are someone with something to say. If you're writing, you're a writer.

"I'll Never Know Enough,
So Why Even Start?"

Cary

HAVE YOU EVER stopped writing in frustration, and said to yourself, "I'll never know enough"?

Think about the last time you had this thought. What did you do next? Did you examine the words that just flitted through your head? Did you ask whether it was a true statement? Or did they send a chill through your blood and stop you cold?

"I'll never know enough" means nothing on its own. It means nothing if we do not ask, "Enough for what?"

Why is the statement meaningless on its own? Because its terms are too broad. Let's take this statement apart. It contains two problematic words, "never" and "enough." "Never" implies infinity, and we don't deal with infinity in Finishing School. We deal in weeks and hours, in months and years, in minutes and seconds, but never in never. Never has no value for us. It can't be divided up into segments any more than zero can. It doesn't have any substance. So we don't even touch it. We let it lie there in its sublime nothingness.

The other problematic word is "enough." This word has no meaning without a context. If we change the statement slightly, to "I don't know enough," then it becomes clear that we need to ask, "Enough for what?"

In Finishing School this is how we combat frustration and the feeling of being overwhelmed. We don't allow words like "never" to cloud our thinking. Rather than say "never" or "sometime," we say "when?" and "for how long?" Instead of saying "enough," we say, "enough for what?"

We work on things that are doable. If we encounter a barrier, we adjust. If something appears impossible, we ask, "What part of this is impossible? How can we go around that part, if it is not possible? How can we adjust the overall project to encompass, or eliminate, this one small part that is impossible?"

For instance, is it impossible to write a historical novel about a boy who befriends Julius Caesar? Of course not. Do you need to be the world's greatest classical scholar to write such a novel? I think not. What concrete elements are needed for a historical novel about a boy who befriends Caesar? What does any historical novel need? It needs a setting, characters, and a story. That's about it. To bring pleasure, these items must be appropriate to the context and believable, but mainly it is a job of avoiding obvious mistakes. No hula hoops. No cell phones.

Rather than saying, "I'll never know enough," ask yourself, "What do I need to know for this story?" This is the material you need to collect. So set about collecting it.

Here is another trap related to the problem of "I'll never

know enough." Some of us simply enjoy finding things out. We like the process of looking things up and examining pictures; we like reading accounts of things that happened a long time ago; we like going into archives and interviewing people. We like hearing their stories. If we carry this too far, we are likely to accumulate more information than we need. This causes two problems. One, we may go on forever gathering information and never finish the work. And two, we may feel compelled, since we have gathered the information, to find someplace to shove it inside the work, even though it doesn't fit or is not needed.

I am one of those people who gathers too much information. Especially if it is from personal experience, I like to try to find a place to put it in what I am writing. Doing this gives me a certain secret aesthetic pleasure. It is like a move in a game that delights me. For instance, I like to say to myself, here I am on Lake Trasimeno, where on June 24, 217 BC, during the Second Punic War, Hannibal defeated the Romans in the biggest ambush in military history.

I don't have to put that in the book. Except I just did! It's an example of something. It's supporting evidence. It is also totally irrelevant, but so it goes. I was talking about something and trotted this out as an example. But it was dangerous because I had to look it up on Wikipedia, and if I hadn't been very careful, I'd still be there, on Wikipedia, instead of here, typing. Because it was an interesting battle. It is also generally considered to have involved the first use in military history of the flanking maneuver. But in the interest of careful time management, I must admit that I spent about fifteen minutes reading basically extraneous material. That time could easily have ended up wasted. I did slip in this bit about Hannibal. But now we're really wasting time and going nowhere. Plus my attention had been diverted. It is a little hard to continue in the former spirit of the piece.

Nota bene: it is a good idea to avoid such distractions wherever possible, to conduct research separately from drafting.

If you are interested in Myers-Briggs personality typology, you might notice that perceiving types tend to enjoy open-ended discovery and research more strongly than, say, judging types.

So in general we can say this about such thoughts as "I'll never know enough": Cognitive scientists have proven experimentally that fleeting thoughts that pass through our minds almost without our noticing can powerfully influence our moods and perceptions. So we need to come up with ways to deal with them and combat their effects. We examine them to see if they are literally true in any way, and if not, to see if they are indicators of something else, either that we are tired and need a break, or that there actually is something we need to discover in the work.

In any case, it is never true that we will never know enough, because the statement itself is flawed. By itself, it means nothing. We always ask: enough for what?

The Bear and the Magpie

Cary

I WAS LEADING a weekend writing workshop in Northern California when a bear walked into the room.

It wasn't a real bear. It was a bear in someone's story, but it appeared so vividly in her story that we could all smell it. The bear was slow moving and fearless. The bear was hairy and warm. It lumbered through, nosing in people's bags. For the woman whose piece of writing that bear entered, he was a messy, implacable manifestation of her own creativity: hungry, passionate, stinky, and dangerous. I do not know who the bear was for the other people in the room, but for me he was a metaphor for the paradox at the heart of writing: *we do not control our creativity.*

In the writer's universe, creativity and control coexist in fruitful tension. We need control in order to write clearly and make sense. But we also need to allow novel, powerful images and memories to float into consciousness. For this, we must relax some control, and relaxing control brings with it a little fear, for as civilized, socialized beings, most of us have developed lifelong habits of mental control. We need mental control to avoid making mistakes and being scolded or suffering embarrassment. We need to watch what we say, think before we speak, consider the feelings of others. Yet to write, at times we must do the exact opposite: We must embody the speech of strangers, children, idiots; we must seriously entertain alien notions. We must vividly reimagine scenes that once were emotionally or physically painful. All these acts, necessary to creative work, require a certain relaxing of control. Thus they require overcoming fear—fear of what might happen, or how we might feel, or how we might be perceived if these thoughts that come unbidden into our minds become known to others.

What I love about the bear is that it evokes the delicious paradoxical twins of terror and love. Also it brings with it the universal fear of being devoured, for the bear is a devouring beast, and so is the great maw of the unconscious—the source of dreams, mysteries, and creative brilliance.

So in this chapter, alert to the contrary tugs of precision and abandonment, I write in a style somewhat "under the influence," not so much providing advice as enacting a drama, the drama of encounter with the life-giving force of the unconscious, or, as I like to call it here, the bear. When we open ourselves to the creative act, we invite a powerful and alien force to wander in and make itself at home. The bear upsets our plans, ignores our schedules, and steals our lunch.

Each of us has an animal world, populated in childhood but still active in reserve. Of all the animals in that world, the bear was chosen to do this work, for the bear appears to the adult psyche as the adult appears to the child: powerful, unpredictable, frightening, but also warm and attractive; one thinks, if only the bear could be domesticated.

When the workshop was over, I brought the bear home with me. I thought it would be great to have a bear, a creature to be the embodiment of all the forces that keep me from my work. Once I identified him, he seemed to be everywhere and into everything. The bear goes where he wants to go. He does not ask questions or pussyfoot around. He slumbers and then wakes up and moves around upstairs or downstairs or outside.

The bear will act in your interest but against your wishes. Sometimes when he shows up he is protecting you. Sometimes he hides your car keys when you're late for a party you do not really want to attend. Sometimes he sends a call to voice mail, telling you something you were not ready to hear. The bear works by preventing me from delving into things that it believes I cannot handle. As adults shield children from sights too gruesome, so the bear shields adults.

The bear is scheming and alarmingly self-confident. The bear thinks he knows what is best. The bear knows that if we can just stay in the woods, away from the humans, we will be okay. So he hides the car keys; he hides our test results. And he gently nudges us to go to church, because he thinks that will help: at least people sit in neat rows, and there is someone in charge.

Sometimes an adult must plead with the bear: Please let me go into the pit with the skulls! Please let me see the gruesome accident scene! Please let me remember the time my mommy hit me with a spatula! Please, bear? It's for my writing. I promise to come back. I promise not to look too long. The bear nods, and the adult goes off with his lollipop, in his short pants, looking for the gruesome scene, and when he gets there the bear has drawn a gauzy curtain across it. But I can't see the welts! I can't see the food on my mother's tooth as she threatens me with the spatula! And the bear smiles, for he has done his job. He knows that humans have limits, even if we do not seem to heed them.

Once I got the bear home, I discovered that he had a cousin seated on his shoulder, a magpie who sat silently enjoying her view of the chaos. When the bear took a rest, she sprang to life. I respected the bear, but the magpie, on the other hand, I could really do without.

The magpie chatters all day long. Whatever exists within us, below our awareness, the magpie reads out loud like the morning news. Caw, caw, caw—or whatever it is—she has seen something frightening and can't forget it and can't let me forget it either and does not know how to calm down. She is in a state of constant alarm, which gives the world, seen through her eyes, the quality of a war zone. I protest, but she says, "Look around you! Are you crazy?"

She says, "Oh, there's no point in sitting there writing when you could be out earning money or finding the love of your life. It's a glorious day. Look at that sunshine. Don't you need new drapes? That old couch needs a new duvet. You could use a haircut. Maybe your friend Beth is at Starbucks having a Frappuccino. You could hear about her date with the Polynesian. There are walnuts in the fridge. You could make a walnut cake. I wonder how the Mets are doing. Have you watered the plants? Why not make a cup of coffee and go out on the balcony? Oh, look, there's Facebook!"

And she is sometimes the frightened child warning me *not* to go outside. But unlike the bear, she has no guile. Underneath, of course, like the bear, she is simply frightened for me, which is projection, for she is frightened for herself, for she has been traumatized by what she has seen: the fires of Auschwitz, the depredations of priests, the way a needle in an arm spells a life gone to dirt, how an afternoon hungover in the hot shadows of an urban June can be its own kind of hell: she has seen all this and can't sit still.

Like the bear, the magpie must be accepted and allowed to do its thing. Sometimes magpie news is real news: it means we are restless or lonely or hungry, and we can meet these needs and then return to writing. The magpie is also a bit of a poet. So be amused, but stay in the chair. One or two interruptions from the magpie need not disrupt your whole day. Let the magpie's eyes fall shut as she perches on her tree limb, watching through the window.

I think one reason Finishing School has at least a fair chance of allowing us to carry out our wished-for work in the face of massive interference from our internal protectors is that once we are used to the routines of Finishing School, we do not wake up the bear and the magpie; they do not even notice what we are up to, because the habit of writing has become orderly and regular. Finishing School does not try to tame the untamable. Rather, we create an orderly system through which our creativity can thrive. Routine quiets the vigilant eyes of my protectors; they go to sleep and snore, like fortress guards in their chairs at the gates of the castle.

Unconscious fears, anarchic inspiration, and magpie voices are simply the conditions within which we work. The only way we could possibly make them entirely still would be to kill them, so we must coexist. The trick is not to get them stirred up. Let sleeping bears lie.

Think of an umbrella. It doesn't stop the rain. It helps us deal with conditions. Whatever else may be going on inside us, we know that if we schedule time and clarify our goals, we will make progress.

The bear has no defense against this, nor does the magpie.

The schedules and plans we create in Finishing School are not cages or chains. A creative schedule works more like a bright white surface with grid marks, which makes visible, by contrast, the squiggly profile of our creativity.

I did not realize until I made a schedule and tried to follow it just how blinding are the phenomena of inspiration. By making a weekly schedule for writing and trying to follow it, we discover just how many obstacles there are and just how strange and wily our own hidden impulses can be. The point is, by setting out on a rational path we discover the exact degree to which we are irrational. Once we have discovered this, we need no longer be troubled by it. Our irrationality is just a condition, a kind of weather.

What I am saying is that we harbor great powers within us. They can be helpful or they can mislead us. We cannot tame them. They can provide the rich texture of dreamlike prose or they can lure us into fruitless wandering in the aisles of IKEA. But we can order our lives to make room for them. And we can learn to recognize when they are leading us astray. We do this by envisioning and proclaiming what we want, and then calmly taking note of just how far, each week, the bear and the magpie encourage us to stray from our dreams or attempt to protect us from them, to make us turn away. We make constant course corrections as we steer toward the stars.

Judgment
"Whose Judgment Do I Fear, and How Can I Proceed in Spite of It?"

The Special Problem of Telling the Truth About Your Family

Danelle

AS WITH EVERYONE else I've met in Finishing School, I came to class because I could not get over a hump in my writing. After decades as a journalist writing other people's stories, I felt inhibited when I wanted to write about my family.

Family is a religion with its own tenets, parables, and saints. Without faith, the whole thing starts to crumble. When you write, you are a heretic. You call out the ceremonies as false and say the foundational beliefs are myths. If you have the courage and the skill to convey things exactly as you see them, you may be thrown out of the temple, forced to wander the world alone. In writing, you have drawn attention to something that others deny, perhaps disgraced a father in front of his children. If what you write gets published, the ripples it will cause may disrupt family gatherings for years. When you compress these consequences, it is no surprise that they form an enormous barrier to finishing.

The family is an audience you know well. You hear them in your head as you work. You can imagine this one's or that one's reactions to each sentence. Writing often stalls while you mount defenses to imaginary critiques. In Finishing School I have seen writers struggle with choosing a point of view that allows them to speak most freely. Many experiment with switching eras: the adult looking back, a wise teenager, the child. If you are writing from the view of childhood, the reader may grant you the credulousness of innocence and forgive some exaggeration. If you are writing about your siblings or other family peers, you don't get this free pass. What brought me into Finishing School was the trouble I was having with writing about my daughter.

My daughter dropped out of college, three-quarters of the way through her freshman year, to hop trains. She spent a year and a half living on the streets and snagging meals out of Dumpsters as she moved from Oregon to Austin to New Orleans, then to Jacksonville and Nashville, and back to New Orleans. Occasionally she'd call from a moving train, unsure of what state she was in. Often she lost her phone, and I kept a list of all the numbers she'd called me from. After each phone call, I wrote what I remembered and how I felt. The journal was solace and record keeping in case we had to find her.

When she came home, after a year and a half on the rails, our relationship seemed fragile, and I was careful not to ask too many questions. A year after she returned, eight young train hoppers, some of whom she knew, died in a squat fire in New Orleans. I thought if I wrote about them, I might be able to understand my daughter better, but it would be a difficult story to report on my own. I knew I would never be admitted into this underworld unless she served as my guide.

I asked her if she would come with me to work on the story, and to my surprise she agreed. Two weeks after the fire we went to New Orleans, and we returned twice more that year. She led me down ravaged streets where more than half of the homes were abandoned, to the warehouse ruins where the eight had died, and into squats without running water or electricity, where we crouched on the floor as I interviewed her friends. There was a wild night at the St. Roch Tavern, where a young man celebrating his birthday showed me how he played pool using his erect penis as a cue. On a humid night in May, we were invited to a cookout on a desolate block. As dinner was served, I was treated like a queen. Someone scrounged up a chair for me to sit on, and someone else contributed a real plate and cutlery for my meal, as the chaos around us escalated. There were young men jousting on bikes, a wrestling match on the asphalt, and several people shooting up in the archways of abandoned apartment buildings. Eventually the cops came, and my daughter and I jumped in the rental car and sped away, with her directing me in how to take evasive action as we swerved through the Ninth Ward like girlfriends on a spree.

I assumed when I started the squat fire story that the sixty thousand words I'd written in my journal would form its spine. I'd juxtapose the things I had felt when my daughter was away with the experiences of the parents of the young people who died. The writing in my journal was rich because it was raw. I got a thrill reading entries that had been written in real time. But as I interviewed the parents and friends of those who had died, I saw that I didn't need my journal. The story was not about my pain, and the sentiments in my journals were not unique to me. The feelings I shared with the other parents were best expressed by those mourning their losses, not through the perspective of one anticipating a loss that did not come. My journal helped me know what questions to pursue, but in the eight-thousand-word article I used about five hundred words about my daughter and me.

The story about the squat fire was a success, and I appeared on several radio shows to talk about it, including one with my daughter. The hosts questioned me about her, but I steered the focus to the people in the article. After interest in that story died down, I continued reporting on crime on the rails, gangs, rail cops, and the business of trains. I saw the potential for a good book there. In the time since the publication of the squat story, I had gained perspective on what my daughter and I had done to heal our relationship when we were in New Orleans, and I saw that story as part of the book.

I opened my journal, thinking again that this was the place to start, but what I found there made me wince. In the journal I was heartbroken in my certainty that my daughter dropped out of college because she did not respect me or trust me, and that she had rejected the way I saw the world. Reading it four years later, I could see how wrong I had been. In taking me into her life on the rails, into her secrets, and trusting me to tell the story of her and her friends, she had proven that what I had written in the journal was not true.

The words of writer and teacher Joyce Maynard kept coming back to me as I found myself unsure of how to start. She has said that when writing about the family you should "write as if you are an orphan." I wanted to feel that free, to be bold, and dare to say it all, but that encouragement seemed cruel in writing about my child. Writing as if my daughter were dead did not offer me freedom. Rather it made me doubt that I should visit this topic a second time. If I wrote about this again, how far back into my daughter's life should I go? Weren't the stories of her childhood hers to tell, not mine? Didn't I have an obligation to protect her privacy? Or at least to ask her for permission? My daughter had granted me this license once. She could rescind it. Was it not her right to say to me, "Enough! Get over it, Mom, and move on." Every time I got to that part of the book proposal, I was stumped. This is what brought me into Finishing School.

In Finishing School, Cary honored my problem rather than solving it. He suggested that I wasn't so much blocked as struggling with big issues. Taking on this topic, writing about something where there was so much at stake, was causing me to reckon with the harm I could cause. Fiction writers face these issues too, but I had made my job tougher by implying that what I was writing was the truth. True for me, but perhaps not true for my daughter. This had raised many ethical and aesthetic problems and, in this way, it was bringing out the best in me. "Balancing emotions results in the best first-person performance," Cary said, and I jotted the words down in my notebook. He talked about being respectful of the nuances of words so I could convey precisely what I needed to say. What was so soothing about his remarks was that he instantly flipped my mood about my fitful progress. I was not a Bigfoot smashing the feelings of anyone who got in the way of my work, nor was

I a failure, lazy, or dumb. I was a writer wrestling with a tough writing problem, and I was asking all the right questions.

Wrestling does not seem like writing. It seems like stalling, as if you are too timid to allow yourself to express the things you feel and perhaps too timid to even feel what you feel. When something profound has happened to you, it may seem easier not to think about it. However, writers know that if you avoid it, it controls you. You cannot let it out, and you can't think about it unless you give yourself permission to go all the way. Giving yourself leeway to be as ugly and unpleasant as you feel, to release the pain completely, is a frightening amount of freedom. It's as if you are too frightened of your power. It's not just the fear of saying it all that inhibits you but the idea that if you do you may strafe the landscape and leave no vegetation standing because what you have to say is such a blast of fire. In the writer's mind, the prospect of that destruction creates its opposite, a timidity about saying anything at all.

As my journal showed me, that raw voice seems very empowering and honest, but that power is short-lived. Having a score to settle can generate some really terrible writing: sloppy, one-sided. Outrage is a good motivation to write, but you cannot stay in a voice of revenge and keep readers interested. When I reread my journal, I saw that the writing that was bitter and condescending was tedious. I was grateful that I had my journal, because in it I had not tried to second-guess how I felt. In some passages a phrase seemed perfect, some sentences had great rhythm and others recorded some details that, in retrospect, had more meaning than I was able to detect at the time. Most of what I wrote there was not useful to the writing I was about to begin. The ratio of using five hundred words of the six thousand struck me as being just about right, but I was extremely grateful I had recorded how I felt in real time, because of what it showed me about writing about the family.

As the journal showed me, there are many shadings of the truth, and what seemed true, was true, and felt true changed places over the years. This is not to say that I should belittle my experience but that I should question and question again whether I am merely drawing attention to myself rather than serving the reader and the story. Having a score to settle can sneak up on you, as it did in some pages of my journal. In some descriptions my word choice dripped with bitterness, and this caused me to doubt my narration. I quickly found that voice tiresome, and so would readers.

Reckoning with the raw emotion of the journal helped me to become more comfortable with the feeling that I also had a story to tell. When something traumatic happens in a family, each member has a right to a point of view. My daughter pulled herself away from the family, from me, in a most dramatic way. Her reasons are her own. That is her story to tell, if she chooses to tell it, in whatever expressions she finds. I've heard hints of it in the songs she writes, one of which assails her father and me. I have my story too. As long I continue to question my motives and search, to the extent that I am able, to be fair, I should not be afraid to tell it.

In the religion of the family, my journal showed, I saw myself as a saint and as a martyr. I had only been good, never bad, so why had this happened to me? Seeing myself in this lofty position, I chose to write my journal in a voice that was brave and bold and tolerant, disciplined too—the voice of someone who held out hope and had faith befitting my saintliness. And while this was a part of what I experienced, after what I learned about my daughter and myself as we made our way through the streets of New Orleans, it no longer felt like the most interesting part of what happened, nor even much worth writing about. The special problem of writing about the family is that it has powerful and immediate consequences, and because of that, it takes more time and good judgment to understand what you truly feel.

The Winchester Mystery Novel: Denying Mortality by Endlessly Revising

Cary

IN 1995 I wrote and published a short story called "When Life Was Wild," and then I kept on writing beyond the short story, and at a certain point I began to call what I was writing a novel because it was long and kept going and had a lot of words in it. It was long and had a lot of words in it and was about the same people and the same setting and situation as the short story, so I was calling it a novel, but there was a problem.

Things happened in this novel for no apparent reason. You didn't know where you were in time and space, and, sometimes, who was talking was a mystery. You had to wonder who the main character was and how the author felt about her or him and what the main conflict might be and why people were doing what they were doing.

In 1884 a psychic told Sarah Winchester, widow of the gun magnate William Winchester, that as long as she continued to add more rooms to her home she would be able to keep the ghosts of those who had been victims of her husband's guns at bay. She began building immediately and without a plan: stairways to nowhere, odd-shaped rooms, a crazy labyrinth no one dared wander through lest they get lost. Construction continued without interruption until her death on September 5, 1922. The house is now a popular San Jose tourist attraction.

In these two events, more than one hundred years apart, a similar human drive was at work: the drive to deny mortality.

It may be that Sarah Winchester consciously believed she could defeat death in this way, but I think it was probably something slightly more complicated: that because she could not admit to herself that her time on earth was limited, she did not see the urgent and pressing need to bring her project to a close. She and I are alike in that during this period of my life I saw no need to stop writing and make something useful and comprehensible of this thing I had started to call a novel. I was living in my own denial of death, endlessly constructing this mythical town that had formed in my mind.

In 2009 I had been doing this for fourteen years, writing without direction, adding rooms as I went, with no central narrative and no end state in mind.

Then one Friday afternoon I received a phone call from my physician telling me that I had a very rare form of bone cancer, called chordoma, which was slowly eating away the base of my spine.

My first thought on receiving this phone call was, "Now I really do have to finish that novel."

There is a common thing people say about artists, that they seek immortality through their work, but I think the truth is a little more subtle. Immortality is unattainable. Making good work that has lasting impact is quite doable. Knowledge of our own mortality helps us work more passionately in the here and now. If mortality is not right up in my face, I will take life for granted. I will pursue childish amusements and shallow satisfactions. Only when my face is pushed into the sidewalk and the boot is on my neck do I remember, "Oh yeah, the clock is ticking while I write my amusing journal speculations and anecdotes." There is a difference between writing journal entries and publishing a novel, and if I am honest with myself, I want to publish the novel. And I have to do that before I die because afterward is too late. It's as simple as that.

So while I do not know about the mental state of Sarah Winchester, I do understand the appeal of a project for which there is no apparent end.

I also understand how a shocking phone call can focus the mind wonderfully. Before that call from the doctor, I had been writing this tale mainly for amusement and solace, with the thought that one day it might somehow turn into a novel. I had been writing what Danelle and I jokingly call "the Winchester mystery novel."

To be fair, when I started writing in this way, in 1995, I was not just a happy, oblivious soul. I was a tortured underling doing a faceless, meaningless temp job in a faceless corporation. I was using writing as a form of solace. But I was only half honest about my ultimate purpose, because in my fantasies what I was writing was going to turn into a novel.

But how?

Oh, somehow. It'll all come together. If I just keep writing, I told myself, it'll all come together.

Maybe in 150 years. But I didn't have 150 years and that was the message of my wake-up call from the doctor.

Now, I would like everybody to get that wake-up call. You don't have 150 years. It's not going to just come together. If you're writing endlessly without a structure and without an ending, and you think it will come together, think again.

What if you only had a year to live? Would you change your approach?

I've heard of an exercise people do where they imagine their own funeral, and I'll bet it's pretty useful. I never did it as an exercise. I did it in the doctor's office. I did it on the phone that Friday afternoon, and what I heard mourners saying about me was, "Well, he was a pretty talented writer but he could just never get it together to finish that novel."

Fuck!

I just don't want people saying that about me after I'm gone.

It's not about immortality. I know I'm not living forever. That's exactly the point. It's about dying.

There was a purpose to the writing I was doing while riding a San Francisco streetcar five days a week, to and from a tedious, exhausting corporate job. This daily, unstructured writing was helping to keep me sane. So I understand the urge to write freely, without a clear plan. Such writing is not without its pleasures and rewards. Maybe doing such writing is keeping you sane too through a difficult time.

But there came a time when I had to find the hidden crystalline structure within this mass of words. There came a time to give meaning to the meandering. And that was getting the cancer diagnosis.

In 2011, two years after that diagnosis, I had undergone a grueling surgical resection and two months of radiation and was back working again full time at Salon.com, writing the "Since You Asked" advice column. Facing death had changed me. I was no longer the carefree person who assumed things would work out in their own time. This thing I had been calling a novel was in terrible shape, but I wanted to get it into shape and publish it. I wanted it to be read by others. I had lost my way in its labyrinthine hallways and I knew I needed help.

So I searched the Internet for writing conferences, and I found one near San Francisco that sounded just annoying enough that it might be what I needed. It was called the Write to Market workshop, and if there was anything stupider sounding or anything I wanted to do less than "write to market," I didn't know what it was, so of course I immediately applied, paid good money, and went there.

Before I arrived I had to fill out a questionnaire. One request was, "Please give us a sample of your protagonist's interior monologue." I looked at all the many words I had written over the many years of writing this novel and realized I did not have such a thing. I had no "protagonist's interior monologue." So I made one up. Incidentally, to write my protagonist's interior monologue I had to decide who my protagonist was. I picked the most interesting, compelling figure, and then realized, "Okay, she must be the protagonist!" That's how ignorant I was about my own novel. I wasn't even sure who the protagonist was. Then, once I realized she was my protagonist—which would have been obvious all along had I realized how completely, utterly foundational it was to know—I had to get inside her skin and create her voice. So I did.

Once I wrote from inside her head, I realized that up until that point I had been regarding her from outside, turning upon her what we might call without irony "the male gaze."

This experience, though humbling, was useful. The other sample the questionnaire asked for was my "elevator speech." Elevator speech? Please, kill me. How dare someone ask me to sum up my novel in two sentences? It's so much bigger than that! You have no idea! It's gargantuan! You can't sum it up like that! Plus I had to deliver this pitch in front of living human beings. Out loud. The thought still makes me gag. But it helped.

So if you too are writing a long, meandering "novel" with no clearly articulable premise, I highly recommend taking as much time as you need to come up with a pitch. Once I found the right pitch, it was like a feng shui treatment for my Winchester mystery novel. It exerted a force of gravity on the surrounding pieces, bringing order.

I am still sometimes amazed that I found the courage to go to the conference. What is it that drives us, after years of avoidance, to finally take action? For that matter, I might ask, what has driven you to pick up this book? Do you too have a persistent, nagging sense that you need to complete some project before time runs out? Perhaps fate is knocking on your door too. Fate has a way of backing you into a corner where you have no choice but to face things.

In my case, I have to say, I finally took action because inaction was just too uncomfortable. It was emotional pain. It was fear of things turning out badly. It was fear of repeating my father's mistakes, fear of missing out, fear of growing old full of regrets and wasted opportunities. It was fear of people at my funeral saying, you know, when it came down to the wire, he just didn't have it.

In his Pulitzer prize–winning 1973 book *The Denial of Death*, Ernest Becker showed how underlying almost every human endeavor is a fundamental drive to deny our own mortality. The things we buy, the houses we live in, the food we eat, how we educate and raise our children, why we create art—all these human endeavors have at their core a drive to overcome or deny the inescapable fact that one day each of us will die and all traces of us will vanish from this earth.

In Becker's view, this fact is simply too much for the human psyche to bear, too much to contemplate, and thus our attempts to deny this fact form the driving force behind much of our symbolic behavior.

So I got that phone call from the doctor in 2009 telling me I had cancer, and the first thought that popped into my head was that I had to finish this novel I had been working on for fourteen years—and does that make any rational, medical sense at all?

No. It makes sense only if we accept the idea that our creative endeavors are, among other things, fueled by our denial of death.

But there is a paradox here.

Because we fear death, we deny death. Because we deny death, we pretend time is limitless. Because we pretend time is limitless, we feel we can always get around to our project later. Because we feel we can get around to our project later, we never do it. Because we never do it, we lose our shot at immortality, and we become unhappy and don't know why we can't do it, and we begin to hate ourselves and seek psychotherapy.

Or, alternatively, we go to Finishing School.

And what do I want? Why am I doing this apparently fruitless thing—trying to finish a novel so there is something that lives beyond me? I don't want to live forever. I just want people to know I was here. I want them to know how much beauty there was, how much struggle, how much pain. And that's why I couldn't shrug it off when I faced the prospect of leaving this planet before my time was up. I just want people to know I was here.

Furthermore, I don't think building the Winchester Mystery House or writing the Winchester mystery novel is as much an effort to defeat death as it is a consequence of not facing death, a consequence of a denial that's already in place. It may seem like a subtle difference, but it's a big difference to me. Because if you really face your inevitable disappearance from this planet and all its beauty and all the people in it whom you love and who love you, you know you can't achieve immortality. All you can do is make good work so that people know you were here, and you can only do that if you shape your work so it can be packaged and disseminated. If you write endlessly without structure or purpose, no publisher will buy it and no reader will read it. After you're dead, it will remain wherever you left it. Your relatives may find it in a drawer and see that you had a flair for words. But it will not become a voice that speaks from beyond the grave.

So think about it. You may be writing in times of stress to save your soul; you may be using a journal to make your hidden thoughts visible to yourself; you may be toying with fiction and poetry. But if behind this practice is a burning desire to make something known to the world, to leave a mark, not because it makes you immortal but just because you want people to know you were here and to speak your name after you are gone, then you may be ready to get to work assembling, in an orderly way, something that can live beyond you.

Not because you think you can be immortal. On the contrary: because you know you're going to die.

Six Signs That You May Be Writing the Winchester Mystery Novel

There are lots of other reasons a novel can take too long. There could be deep psychological reasons why you do not want to end it. Here are some things to look for while you try to figure that out.

1. You don't know how the book ends.

If you don't know how the book ends, you can keep writing, hoping to get to an end, but you might just keep writing forever, and that would make the wait for your second book a very long one indeed.

2. You have been working on it for more than five years.

Five years is a long time. It's a whole college education long. It's more than a whole presidential term long.

3. You have no outline.

An outline causes you to think in an architectural way, and if your problem is that you are too focused on the luxurious experience of letting the words flow onto the page in a rapturous cascade, attempting and failing to write an outline will start up that part of your brain that looks at Earth from outer space.

4. You cannot express the nugget of the book in a sentence or two. In other words, you have no pitch.

When I finally found the pitch, it changed my life. It really did. Then I could stay focused on exactly what the novel was about. Every page is about that. Plus it saves me lots of embarrassment and shame. I used to launch into long attempts at explanation when people asked me, and I would talk too much and end up feeling stupid and ashamed of my inability to simply explain what my novel was about. Now I just say, "It's about a punk runaway who becomes America's biggest sitcom star." I usually don't have to say more than that.

5. You are rewriting and perfecting scenes rather than moving forward with the story.

Stop reworking scenes. Move forward with the story. Do jump cuts. Stop describing where people are if what they are doing isn't changing the world or causing them to be put in danger or making people laugh. Stop describing what they are wearing if they are not going to a party, and only let them go to a party if something will happen there to change the direction of their lives. Tighten it up! Get it moving! Make things happen!

6. There are lots of secondary characters with long backstories.

Describing many secondary characters with long backstories can bog you down. Let some of the backstories go. Move forward in time.

"It's All Been Said Before, So Why Bother?"

Danelle

WHEN THE WRITING seems lifeless on the page and efforts to revive it are futile, you may decide that the whole project is pointless. Your words sound like so many others you've read over a lifetime. How can you, with your regular life and modest skills, say something original about a sunset? Or marriage? It's all been said before, said by better people—people better educated, smarter, or more in touch with how they feel. So much has been said, and, as we know, most of what we read is garbage. Billions of words published every year, thousands of books, many of them bad, many never read. Why add your babble to the cacophony?

When I was failing at writing a novel more than a decade ago, this frame of mind was mine. I had been bitten by the idea that I was going to knock out a murder mystery set in Hollywood. I was working at *People* magazine in Los Angeles, and I had experienced plenty of outrageous true-life incidents with celebrities that I wanted to dramatize. After a year I had a hundred pages that contained some funny scenes, but nothing tied the book together. The murder that was supposed to motivate the plot seemed tacked on, extraneous to the comings and goings of the protagonist (a thinly disguised me). As a result, the book felt off center: falsely jaunty and too clever. I wanted to abandon it, but it was the piece of writing I'd put the most of myself into, so I also did not want to let it go.

I fell into an even deeper funk when, around that time, a Jungian psychologist published a controversial book called *The Seven Basic Plots*. Christopher Booker had spent decades analyzing fiction in all its forms, everything from the *Odyssey* to *Four Weddings and a Funeral*, to identify the seven essential sequences of events at the heart of fiction. I rushed to the bookstore to buy it the same day I heard about it, thinking that if I just picked one of his plots and stuck to it, all decisions about the book would be easy because I would have a formula to follow.

At the bookstore, I discovered his book was more than seven hundred pages long, a heavy lift compared to my breezy expectations. I leafed through it, still looking for a quick fix. Booker began by dividing all characters' actions, independent of plot, into four stages: the anticipation stage, the dream stage, the frustration stage, and the resolution. That sounded like me trying to write the novel: dreaming it, anticipating it, getting frustrated. Only I was missing a resolution. *The Seven Basic Plots* was displayed alongside another dreary reduction of creativity, *The Thirty-Six Dramatic Situations*. Seven plots! Thirty-six dramatic situations! Maybe if I just tossed them in the word processor and pressed On, it could come up with a story for me.

The way these books reduced the passionate act of writing to numerical certainties lent creativity a manufactured feel. It also made me feel like an outsider, and not in a good way. The idea that there was this formula that others knew but I did not made me feel incompetent, and that I should stick to short-form journalism. The contradictory nature of my responses just made me more confused. On the one hand, if there was a formula, the dream of saying something original and fresh was hopeless.

Describing this state now, it seems no surprise to me that I have not touched those one hundred pages in almost a decade.

The stress we visit on our work often seems to come from our terror of the judgment of others, when it is our own judgment we truly fear: fear of seeming derivative and that we won't be able to fulfill the requirements of the form. If I do something different, then I'm wrong, but what if I'm not smart enough to know when I'm being derivative? Were all the writers I admire—and even those I disdain—basically laboring in a cliché factory where the human condition could be reduced to seven simple sentences? What is the point of putting myself through all this agony and separation from the world if the end result will just sound like any one of a dozen, or a hundred, novels or stories I've read and been influenced by? Unless the thing I am writing is wholly original and groundbreaking in some way, why do it? I took that one momentary reaction of disgust with my work and ran down a long path to my worth-lessness, with vigorous arguments in support of my mediocrity.

I am not original. I am just like everybody else and therefore I have nothing unique to say.

This problem arose again when I was working on the chapter "The Special Problem of Telling the Truth About Your Family." A friend said dismissively, "Phillip Lopate already said everything that can be said about writing about your family." With all due respect to the impressive intellect of Phillip Lopate, what does that matter? Many books have been written about grief, infidelity, family dysfunction, and friendship. What the reader is drawn to is the world created by the writer and the unique way a particular individual describes that world. It may be that different writers, in describing their experiences, come to similar conclusions, but that does not mean their work is redundant. The contribution you make is to add your perspective and experience. If you get to the same place another writer did, how you got there is what the reader cares about, and what you should care about too. Should the fact that others have written about fears related to writing about their families stop you from adding what you uniquely have to say?

Your job as a writer is to say as truthfully as you can what you see and how you feel. Writing is a high-wire act. It's best not to look at the other circus performers but to attend to the wire.

Arrogance

"How Does Arrogance Blind Me to What Must Be Done?"

"Actually, It's a Trilogy"

Danelle

IT WAS VALENTINE'S Day and I was standing with a writer friend at a bar because we didn't want to be in our apartments facing the obvious truth that we were alone. We ended up at a table with a man and his female friend from out of town. When the man found out that we were writers he got very excited to tell us about his novel, an idea that came to him right after he graduated from college. The idea was for a dystopian science fiction novel where a catastrophic event caused millions to die and only a few with a special quality survived, to live in a hellscape governed by brutish and swift-changing rules. He ended his detailed, densely worded description with a triumphant "Actually, it's a trilogy."

When writers say, "Actually, it's a trilogy," chances are good that not even one book will be written.

True, some books are best told at great length because the world of the novel evolves over decades and even in the decades before the main characters were born. The man at the bar might be correct that this story, if fully unfurled in the hands of a passionate and dedicated writer, would best be told in three linked novels rather than one.

And who am I to squash someone's writing dream? I'm the one who encourages people to write. I believe people are happy when they are writing and can escape into a world of their creation. The act of creativity makes the regular world more bearable. So, writer to writer, I asked him how far along he was in the writing. He looked away and then he looked at me, then he looked away again and said, "I haven't actually started it."

The problem is to write one book, or, to be more exact, the problem is to write one sentence, and then another until you've got a paragraph, and then another paragraph after that until you've built a chapter.

To say that you have an idea not just for a book but for a trilogy makes that one good sentence seem so insignificant that it is almost not worth writing. The trilogy concept may defeat you before you begin.

Thinking of it as a trilogy is probably the chief reason this man hasn't started the book and didn't start it twenty years ago when he was just out of college and the idea was fresh. In aspiring to write a trilogy, especially as your first work, you are saying that your ideas as so big and sweeping, so rich and complex, that they cannot be contained in a single volume. This is why saying you are writing a trilogy is so ambitious as to be a work-killing form of arrogance.

In the course of writing we end up facing our fears and shortcomings. Arrogance like that of the trilogy writer is a way of leaping over that confrontation with inadequacy by having a grander goal, as if only the grandest of goals were worthy of the effort required to write. In setting a goal that big, the writer may think the grandeur of the ambition will create a powerful work ethic and inspire a sense of a mission that needs to be fulfilled. In reality the fears and shortcomings end up having more power than they would have if the goal was to write just a simple sentence and build one sentence upon another, with humble and consistent attention to the craft, until enough was written to step back and assess what you'd managed to create.

Our dreams may be big, and the best dreams are much bigger than we are. The way to address these writing dreams is to come to them as a novice who understands that he or she has a lot to learn along the way. When you start out writing, you may be proud of the way you see things, you may have a story that is burning up inside you and that you want to tell, and you may have a soaring feeling every time you think you might get it done if you work hard enough and do not give up. This pride, linked to a humble sense of how much lies ahead in achieving the dream, is the best combination for completing your work.

"I'm Willing to Be Judged, but Only If I'm Judged the Victor"

Danelle

When I hand over my work to someone for feedback, all I want to hear is praise. Although I've convinced myself that I want an honest reaction, I secretly, strongly, hope that honest reaction is a rave. I want the person who reads it to be astonished by my skills, quote phrases back to me from memory, and describe how she was unable to put it down and read late into the night.

Unfortunately, what we usually get back is a handful of measured compliments followed by a list of things that don't work. That's why criticism is so hard to take. We've set ourselves up for the opposite, hoping the criticism will be light, but it rarely unfolds that way. Or it may be light, but because we were hoping for no criticism at all, every tiny observation that falls short of praise hits like a sharp blow.

The moment when we have decided to expose our writing to the world, it is at its apex. Likely we've settled a lot of the early problems and have corrected some errors that, looking back, seem so obvious we may wince at the memory of those clumsy words on the page. At this apex, we are also at our most vulnerable. The eyes of the person we show it to may be the first, besides ours, to see this work. Handing over the manuscript, or pressing Send on the e-mail that contains the file, is a moment of pride and exhilaration followed by what seems like an unending period of worry. Why isn't the reader getting back to me? What is taking her so long? She's not getting back to me because she's so revolted that she doesn't know what to say. No, it's because she read the first page and is so disgusted she doesn't want to go on. You know what? She's not going to be my friend anymore. That's it. We're through. If she can't treat me with respect, then it was never a real friendship anyway. I'm going to go over there and rip that manuscript from her hands and tell her off.

MAYBE YOU DON'T feel this way as you await feedback, but if you don't, you're among a handful of self-confident writers who already have been working on thickening their skin.

I've been receiving feedback for decades as a journalist, but we don't call it feedback in the newsroom. In book publishing they call it notes. Notes. Sounds so benign when they say "notes," as if they could almost be love notes with little parcels of candy attached, but they are not. In the newsroom, I don't remember that they had a word for it. Most times the editor or the copy editor would just stand up and bellow out my name: "Morton, what the hell is this?" or "Morton! Get over here!" I thought the bruising atmosphere of the newsroom would

make me a champ at hearing criticism when I worked on longer pieces with less of a deadline, but the opposite was the case.
As I wrote books, I was not just churning out words to meet a
daily deadline. The work I sent to friends and colleagues to
read was something I had worked on for a very long time, and
it came with big hopes.

My skin was not so tough when I awaited feedback on the
first screenplay I'd written, perhaps because I was trying a new
writing genre and my ego was much more exposed than it had
been in writing daily news stories. My friend came to me with
a printout of the screenplay that he had marked up with Post-it
notes, a great unfurling of various colors of Post-its that looked
like the plumage of a bird. He is a very organized man, something I like very much about him. He had a different color
Post-it for each kind of error. If it was a plot point that didn't
make sense, that was green. The clumsy dialogue was yellow,
etc. Just looking at the multitude of issues gave me an upset
stomach. When I sat down to go over his critique, I was very
diligent in the beginning, taking meticulous notes on the many
things I needed to correct. As the hour continued, and the fine
points of my failures accumulated, I paid less attention.

When a writer sees that so much is wrong, he or she shuts
down. How could it be so bad? How could I be such a bad
writer? Every fear and insecurity that you have been battling
to get to the point where you have something to share floods
the mind. In some cases, receiving criticism is the last step in
the process because the writer abandons the project after that.

By the end of my friend's critique of my screenplay, I felt
weak and a bit bludgeoned, although I know that was not my
friend's intent. He had spent a considerable amount of time to

read my screenplay thoroughly and reread it with his organized system of Post-it notes, and his goal was to be helpful. He would have been shocked if I told him how upset he made me. This was my fault. I had not discussed with him what would be the most helpful way to deliver his response.

This is a chapter on how to ask for feedback in a way that will not shut down your writing. You must be judged by others if you are going to have your work appear before an audience, and the readers will judge you as well. It is essential that you learn how to handle the remarks people make, remarks that will sting, and the place to start is by sharing your work with people who already like and respect you, because they will be the most mindful of how this will affect you.

You must carefully choose the people who read your work to protect your writing from clumsy and ill-thought-out critiques. The people you choose should be those who like the kind of writing you are doing. Do not show your science fiction novel to someone who likes Jane Austen unless she has demonstrated that she's got taste broad enough to accommodate that genre too. Each kind of writing has its expectations, and the best feedback will come from someone who admires that style and knows the good stuff when she sees it.

In the beginning it is a poor idea to try to get a professional writer to critique your work unless you are paying this person to do it. Writers get solicited often to perform this service for friends and friends of friends, and if they are like me, they feel an obligation to help other writers improve their work. Professional writers are deluged with requests, and reading someone else's work is a time-consuming experience, particularly if you take the responsibility seriously. It's not just the reading;

making a coherent response takes time. And the writer may want additional explanations after he or she gets the response. As the memoirist Mary Karr posted on her Facebook page in 2016, "The number of requests I got last year for people wanting me to read their books exceeded 1000. Please understand I cannot help you with yr manuscript. I have been teaching 30 years, and I read and edit at least 5 former students per month or 60/year. If I accepted 10% of the requests I get, I would be unable to do my own writing and teaching, which I do for money to pay my mortgage—just like you!!!"

Karr brings up a good point about asking nonprofessionals too. Make sure that the person you are asking has time to read this, or work with them to set a deadline for the response. Waiting for your friend to read your work can freeze you in anxiety and produce imaginary arguments in which you criticize them for neglecting you. This is a terrible burden to place on a friendship, and it can cause a rift that will take some energy to repair. If you set a reasonable expectation that your friend agrees to, it takes some of the stress out of waiting for a response.

Make sure you know what you want from this critique. When you hand over your work, it is a good idea to specify that you'd like him or her to focus on the characters' actions and whether they make sense. Or if you are concerned that the dialogue seems a little stiff, ask your reader to keep an eye out for that. Think about what aspect of your work concerns you and make that explicit to your reader, because then the reader will focus on giving you an answer that is most helpful to your progress.

When the time comes to receive the reaction, remember that people communicate clumsily and often say things in an offhand manner that the listener takes deep into the heart. Or they may use a particular word that riles you up, which also can set you back. Cary and I have been reading each other's essays for this book, and early on when I was giving him feedback on one of his, my brusque manner really annoyed him. I was used to the tough and quick world of journalism. I wrote a few comments that started off with "Don't do this, do that." The word "don't" sets off Cary's antiauthoritarian streak. When someone tells him don't, he thinks do. Once we straightened that out—an easy fix—our back-and-forth got smoother.

It was interesting to me that a word that is so casually tossed around in my profession could be taken so differently by a peer, but it revealed how certain phrases provoke a strong response. Most of us don't know what those phrases are for another person, but they often emerge quickly in a feedback session. If your reader says something that you think belittles you or denigrates your attempt to write, you are likely wrong about that. Often a writer holds on to an observation that stung like a blow. The phrase keeps appearing over and over in the writer's mind, taken sometimes as the inspiration for a hostile reaction to the person who said it and at other times like a verdict on the worth of the work. If you find yourself trapped in this spiral of self-defeat, call your reader and ask for an explanation. It is likely that you took what the reader said the wrong way.

Listen for the good and the useful, not for the insults. When giving feedback, your reader will draw your attention to many things, some of which are not useful. A reader might say that she doesn't like this character, and even if you are completely satisfied with the way you wrote him, you may suddenly be confused with doubts. Or you might not be hearing your reader correctly because you are extremely sensitive. Your reader may say something mild, like, "This section is a little unclear and I think you could describe it better." What you hear is, "He thinks I'm a terrible writer and I suck at description." That's not what he said at all, but because of your state of mind, you hear what he said as the worst possible verdict on your work.

When the time comes to receive the response from your reader, remember what you asked your reader to do and listen for the comments that concern that portion. Listen carefully and ask questions if you feel your heart pounding or if you think something your reader said is hurtful. Remember how sensitive you are to this response and how, in that sensitive state, you might not retain the truth of what the reader was trying to say.

And above all listen for the win, not just the loss. Remember the things that your reader said are working, and remember which parts that you think work as well. What you're looking for in a reader's response is a guide to what you need to do next to improve your work. That's what you want to hear, as that is the only part about feedback that is useful.

Last, if the feedback you receive makes you not want to write, bring this problem to Finishing School. Your fellow students and the leader can help you glean from the many remarks your reader made that are useful, which will help you decide where to go next. In Finishing School we address the obstacles that get in the way of our writing and support each other as we face the barriers we build for ourselves and the ones we imagine others are constructing. The class can help you dismantle those and keep you going forward.

"I Don't Need Help; I'd Rather Fail in Secret"

Danelle

SOME WRITERS IMAGINE themselves as lone wolves howling out a singular vision of the world. They believe authenticity comes wild, wide, and untidy. Believing this makes help in any form suspect. A true writer, the myth says, has to work alone and fend off any kindnesses. "I don't want any help," these writers will say, as if help were for losers. As Americans we are raised to suspect dependence as compromise. Independence is prized above many other traits—we do not want to be under the control of others or rely on others' opinions or guidance because those people just might steer us wrong.

True, there are moments when writing pours out of you. Your fingers pound on the keyboard as you try to get it out as quickly as you can. You feel the story writing itself. You've touched a vein, not just inside the body, but through those words on the page, touched a vein of truth about the world. The page is alive, and you can feel that life coursing through your body. For this, you do not need any help.

These times of ecstasy are gifts from the gods of creativity and to be cherished as they happen—and in memory—as they come along infrequently. Everything except these moments is craft: slow, painstaking, emotional-pitfall territory. Those who do not ask for help, or do not acknowledge the help they are getting, even when they do not ask, are unlikely to finish.

The arrogance of the declaration that you don't need help represents a feeling of superiority to all who might offer a bit of support or advice. You may be indignant while protecting your work from the confusing observations of well-meaning friends. If you've ever made an openhearted suggestion to a writer who suffers from this pitfall, you've likely flinched at the condescending snort you got in response. The writer communicates in that gesture that he or she is living life on a higher plane than you, breathing better air, and having more complex reactions than others experience. This is the writer on Mount Olympus, looking down on the rest of us as though we were lesser beings. It's important for a writer to protect the work, and the vision of where it is headed, but you don't have to be an asshole about it.

We all need help to keep going, and we all receive help even if we defend ourselves against it.

Many times you'll make demands on the people around you to protect your solitude, and often you will disappoint them socially. You will duck out on commitments at the last minute because you need to write. If you are married and have children, you're going to need your spouse's help in taking care of the kids so you can write. In asking your spouse in a concrete way to support your dream, you are asking for an endorsement of your work.

You may be grateful to the friends who support your work because they encourage you, and that keeps you going. And, perversely, so do some of those who do not believe you can do it. You're writing because you have something to prove, and these doubters are the ones for whom the proof is needed. I remember when I was a little girl, my grandmother observed me assessing our family with wide and judgmental eyes. "You don't know what you think you know," she said. "I do so," I thought. "I do so." I have always thought that was the moment, at age nine, when I became a writer.

At the moment when we are ready to show our work to others, we need the help of those who agree to read it carefully and are thoughtful in the way they say what they think. Those people help us step back from our role as the lone wolf to wonder, "Does this cry from the heart make sense? Have we said it clearly and in a good sequence?" We need help to know if we've said what we intended to say.

Your writing may be for yourself first, but you want people to read it. And if you get published, you need the help of people you've never met who decide to spend their money and take the time to read what you have to say. You would like it if they would not only buy the work but tell other people they should read it too. We need them to post about it on Facebook and tweet about it so that others have a chance to consider it.

Finishing School helps you remain accountable to your

work. Your creative buddy knows when you pledged to write and for how many hours. And although he or she may know in a general way what you have pledged to do, the specifics quickly fade from your buddy's memory. Your buddy is not looking over your shoulder to see if you are sitting down to work at the appointed hour, but instead generally holding in heart and mind the idea that you are going to write. What you do with those hours is not your buddy's concern. Only that you remain consistent in the commitment, and that you help your buddy fulfill that commitment too.

Anyone who has taken Finishing School knows how powerful this mild accountability is in getting to finish. Knowing that there is someone expecting you to work focuses you. In one Finishing School class, there was a writer who had not touched her novel in ten months. Yet she cribbed some time from the middle of her day at work to try to write something before class because she didn't want to let her creative buddy down. Her buddy had been struggling that week but had still sat down for her hours, and because of that made progress. At work, with her buddy in mind, this writer added another two thousand words, a total of eight thousand words in three weeks. Although she benefited from the defined number of hours and the specific task, the spiritual support of her creative buddy was what inspired her to write with such focus.

FOR PEOPLE BESET with an arrogant attitude, our level, hard-headed, grind-it-out method can be the best medicine of all. No one is going to judge you or argue with you. If you sense in your own blustering that you may not, in fact, be the world's most brilliant writer but are afraid to voice your self-doubts (which are in fact the first glimmers of priceless self-knowledge), Finishing School offers help: a clean, quiet laboratory in which you can explore those thoughts.

The Surprising Upside of Healthy Arrogance: As Revealed by a Teenage Wrestler

Cary

IN JUNIOR HIGH I became a wrestler. On the first day of practice, I got up before sunrise, and my mother made me a high-protein breakfast and drove me to school. For the first couple of weeks, the coach showed us simple holds and how to start a match. Then one morning he had us boys gather in a circle. He asked for a volunteer to enter the ring. Then he asked for a second boy to volunteer to enter the ring and wrestle the first boy. One by one and two by two, boys stepped into the ring and wrestled. The line kept moving. I looked to my left and my right. Some boys were stepping up. Some boys were stepping back. I was waiting for someone else to go. When no one did, I found myself stepping into the ring.

I faced the other boy. We circled. He was much larger than I was. We pawed at each other. I lunged for him, trying one of the moves the coach had showed us. He threw me to the ground. We wrestled. The coach blew his whistle. After we stepped out of the ring, the coach said, "Okay, the boys who have stepped into the ring so far will stay to compete for spots on the team. The rest of you need to seriously think about whether this is right for you. You may keep coming to practice, but you will have to show that you want to be in the ring."

I had been the last one to step into the ring and give it a try. But I had done it. I wanted to be in the ring.

You have to show that you want to be in the ring.

THIS WILLINGNESS TO get into the ring is part of what Danelle and I call "healthy arrogance." I knew when I stepped into the ring that I might look foolish and lose. But I had to take that chance. I had to try it. I had to find out. I didn't think I was that much worse than any of the other scrawny, awkward, pimply, or ridiculously large boys in my class.

I wanted to be in the ring.

Perhaps "healthy arrogance" is not the best term. We could call it courage, nurturing the power motive, appropriate narcissism, or high self-esteem, but "healthy arrogance" captures something darker and more primal in the creative spirit. This is a side that some of us, being the polite, sensitive, artistic types that we are, may prefer not to show. But the truth is, we want our work to be available to others, and making our work available to others means getting into the fray, mixing it up with people who may be far more ambitious, better schooled, more experienced, and perhaps more talented.

It means getting into the ring.

You may get slammed to the mat, as I was. In fact, I was out for several weeks with bruised ribs after that experience. But I never forgot that feeling of going for it, of stepping in, of facing my fears.

According to Stephen P. Kelner's research, detailed in his book *Motivate Your Writing!* the primary motivation of 80 percent of published authors is power.

Holy crap! That explains a lot! Think about the published authors you know. Do you notice something about them? Do you think of it as arrogance or narcissism? It may just be the power motive at work.

Some of us who are just as creative as others seem to get less attention because we aren't out there blowing our own horns. We may have repressed the power motive or not developed it. Maybe we were taught that it isn't seemly to draw attention to ourselves, to seek to influence others, to stand on a hill and shout our message. Yet that is what we need to do if our work is to become known; we may have to elbow others aside, go to the head of the line, and announce our presence.

We have to show that we want to be in the ring.

But it can help to have a playful attitude about it.

WHAT IF YOU said to a friend, "I ate the most amazing meal the other night."

Your friend might reply, "Where was it? Where did you eat?"

"Oh, just this little place. Not well known. Kind of a hole-in-the-wall, actually. I don't think the proprietor is even a professional chef."

"Wow," your friend might say.

"I know. Really. You should try it."

"I'd like to," your friend might say.

So you make a date and pick her up and take her to this place, this little hole-in-the-wall, which also just happens to be your own apartment.

Why can't we talk about our own work with the same enthusiasm with which we talk about the work of others? Do we not love ourselves? Do we not love the work we are doing? Why can't we share that?

We must learn to like our own cooking. That means it has to be good. But it doesn't have to be virtuosic. It just has to be good, so somebody else will want to eat it.

One way to make sure we like our own cooking is to keep it simple and use good, honest ingredients. Living in Italy, I have discovered that it is easy to make a delicious meal if you have good ingredients and you keep it simple.

OKAY, NOW, WHAT if you said to your friend, "I read this poem I really love. I really love this poem. You should read it."

You could show your friend a poem by Wallace Stevens, and she might get it or she might not. Not everybody gets Wallace Stevens's poems, even though he was one of the great geniuses of our age. It can be disappointing when others don't feel about a poem the way you do. You might feel that a gulf in understanding has opened between you.

"You don't get that? You don't see how amazing it is? You really don't? This is obviously a great poem!"

Now, what if you told her, "I just read this poem and I think it's the greatest poem ever!"

"Can I read it?"

"Do you really want to?"

"Sure."

"But what if you don't like it?"

"How could I not like it if you say it's so good?"

"Well, everybody's taste is different."

"I'll be the judge of that. Just show me the poem."

Maybe you show her a Wallace Stevens poem, or maybe you show her one of your poems. Maybe your poem is simpler, more direct, easier to get the essence of. Maybe she likes yours better.

Does that make you a better poet than Wallace Stevens?

MY LITERARY TASTES and opinions have evolved as I have matured. When I was younger, I liked writing that was showy and virtuosic. Lately I have begun to think that the literary models I studied as a young man wanting to become a writer were the wrong ones for me. They were too far advanced for me. They were the products of extraordinary artistic genius and thus beyond my reach—not as an appreciator but as a doer. I could appreciate them but that didn't mean I could do something like them. Was I an extraordinary artistic genius? In the folly of youth, I thought perhaps I might be. After all, somebody has to be the extraordinary artistic genius of his time, no? As a student of literature, I was a bright student. As a scholar I could appreciate the enormous genius of William Faulkner and Vladimir Nabokov, and the poetry of Wallace Stevens. But as a budding craftsperson, I needed models I could emulate. The works of my heroes were not only works of literary genius but of idiosyncratic genius. It would have been smarter to study geniuses whose methods could be emulated.

Who among us will ever do what Wallace Stevens did? We can stand back and marvel, but can we do what he did? His method, apparently, was just to be Wallace Stevens.

When I was really, really young, I got a model rocket at the hobby shop and I thought it could make it to the moon. Why not? I was a kid! This rocket is going to the moon! To me, it was shaped like a rocket and it had fins and a nose cone, so why not?

I didn't understand that what takes a rocket to the moon is inside the rocket.

What took Wallace Stevens's poems to the moon was hidden inside the genius of Wallace Stevens. Believe me, after I got a little older and realized I wasn't taking that rocket to the moon, I still tried. I studied, I memorized, I counted syllables, I followed references, I recited and puzzled and laughed and exhausted myself and fell asleep with *The Palm at the End of the Mind* on my chest. I worshipped those poems. I studied the man, his movements, his life, his letters. But I never got to write like Wallace Stevens. He was an idiosyncratic genius whose methods arose from deep within an opaque and mysterious consciousness.

I couldn't see how it was done. I wasted a lot of time writing poor imitations of Wallace Stevens poems. I now believe it is better to study a writer whose methods we can learn and practice, like Ernest Hemingway or James M. Cain or Charles Simic or Patricia Highsmith. It's not that they are lesser geniuses. But it is possible to study their methods and emulate them. If you look closely, you can understand how their work functions.

Much stylistic genius lies in simplifying. When you are at peace with yourself, simplification comes easily. If you are anguished, embittered, frightened, vacillating between egomania and self-hatred, your work is likely to betray elements of your confusion and chaotic emotion. Finishing School is not psychotherapy, but there is something healing about coming to earth, admitting where you are in your work, reaching out for help and in turn helping others, and making regular, steady progress in your craft. There is peace to be found in humility and a good-humored view of your own strengths and weaknesses, in an appreciation for just how many hours it takes to form a good paragraph or a good page. There is humility and peace to be found even in seeing just how brutal and cutthroat the world is, in seeing how easily we can be thrown to the mat by a stronger foe, in seeing that even if we are thrown to the mat, the mere attempt was ennobling.

We got into the ring.

I would even go so far as to say that what we do when we allow ourselves to go about developing our creative lives in a sober and orderly way is to open a window onto the higher portion of ourselves.

I MIGHT EVEN say that within each of us dwells an echo of the divine, some small shard or remnant of the perfection, beauty, and dignity of the universe, and that our creative striving is in part an effort to reach and revivify that remnant of perfection and beauty. I do not think it is arrogance to regard oneself as holy, imbued with divinity, for each of us is made of the stuff of stars. Each of us is an irreducible combination, the sum of which is life.

To fully celebrate one's own life may in itself be considered arrogant, but it is in fact only a humble acknowledgment of the facts: we are in fact miraculous.

You MUST LEARN to love your own work if you are to take it into the world with joy rather than shame. If you can learn to simplify, you can learn to love your own work, for your work does not have to be the work of Wallace Stevens to have value and to be appreciated. If you can put a few simple, good-tasting ingredients together, you can do just fine. You don't have to write like Nabokov or Wallace Stevens. You can just write like yourself. Just make sure that you yourself really like it—not just because it's yours, but because you have gathered good ingredients and combined them carefully. If it takes time, it takes time. At least you are on the path. And if you are in Finishing School, you have people on your side, reminding you that this is not heedless effort, nor is it shameless arrogance or selfish indulgence.

You are just stepping into the ring.

IF YOU CAN learn to love the simple truth of your own life, your own observations, your own consciousness, the pictures in your own mind unadorned by the festoons and gewgaws of idolatrous ego, unfancied up by poses of superficial brilliance, unperfumed for the ball but straight from the field, dripping perhaps with the sweat of hard labor, muddy perhaps with the mud of the fields, if you can learn to love the simple nourishing products of your own simple heart, maybe you can learn to love your own work, and then you can confidently invite a neighbor to your banquet, saying truthfully that, for you, it's some of the best stuff you've ever tasted.

Part 2

How It Works

Danelle's Two Months in Finishing School

Danelle

THE FIRST TIME I got paid to write, I was a beat reporter. Newspaper editors were more impressed by an accurate story turned in on time than they were by a nicely turned phrase or a well-chosen word. I liked the challenge and the practical attitude that whatever I turned in was as good as I could make it in the time I had. For this reason, I am a writer who does not fear deadlines. I usually don't have trouble finishing things. This has made me something of a pariah to writer friends who labor over a single sentence for hours.

Little did I know that my slightly condescending sympathy for their struggle would be revealed as hypocrisy when I failed to finish a project of my own.

I've collaborated on fifteen books, three of them best sellers, and written dozens of proposals for books that have sold for hundreds of thousands of dollars. Yet when it came to a project of strong personal meaning to me, I lost that swift certainty. I spent two years writing, and not writing, a book proposal.

A friend who knew how I was struggling offered me an empty apartment in a building he owns in Nyack, New York, for two weeks. I took a plane, trains, and finally a very long bus ride to Nyack, imagining that if I could get away from my place in San Francisco, suddenly all would be clear and obvious. I'm not sure why I was convinced that separating myself from my normal life would visit upon me the heavenly angels of clarity and focus, but I was willing to spend money to invoke those angels. Still, this radical transplantation did not work, and neither did I. Every day in Nyack was agony. I wrote very little and I spent a lot of money on white wine.

In the year after my Nyack disaster, I rented cabins in the woods for weekends, where I tried to pep-talk my way into productivity. As I drove to my mountain retreat, the speech was always the same: "This time you're just going to sit your ass down in the chair and bang it out. You've done it before. You've written a book proposal in a weekend. All you have to do is stop fucking around and write." This pep talk was more like shame talk that placed me in a state of mania. I couldn't write, but I wouldn't let myself leave the cabin and take in the beautiful world around me, because that was a treat reserved for the moment when I finished banging it out—goddamn it.

After two years of false starts, every time I thought about this idea I had loved, I felt terrible. At low moments like those, I was certain I'd never write a book under my own name because I was just too much of a loser. Then I saw Cary's advertisement for Finishing School.

Maybe what I needed was support, something I usually avoid.

I liked the fact that I had to commit to only one month at a time, rather than step into a preexisting writers' group where people had chosen up sides. On a Tuesday evening during the first week in October, I drove from my house, on the opposite side of San Francisco, to where Cary then lived, in a house near the Pacific Ocean. Cary taught other writing classes in his home, which was set up well for that. His living room had lots of chairs with thoughtfully placed lamps, power strips, and side tables, each with bright tile coasters and bowls with extra pencils and pens. When he started the class, he pulled a thick, dark curtain across the archway to the living room, and the session began.

In class that first night, there were six people. Besides Cary and me there was Fay, who was trying to complete a screenplay she'd been working on for several years. Christina, who had written three screenplays and a television pilot, was tackling a new form—a short memoir. George had been working on his science fiction novel in fits and starts for nearly twenty years. And there was a poet who recognized, as Cary talked about the process, that Finishing School was not suited for her, and she dropped the class.

Cary handed us sheets of paper printed with a calendar for the month of October. He asked us to commit to specific times during the week when we would work on our project. He encouraged us to access our calendars on our phones or computers or open our datebooks to identify clear spaces in our schedules for writing time.

Writing down specific times is a big step, seemingly bigger than writing the check to enroll in Finishing School. Committing to write seemed subversive. We were upsetting the normal order of obligations and priorities by claiming in advance that this time would be devoted to writing. I am paid for my journalism and my collaborations on nonfiction books. Writing this book proposal would be time spent on something that wasn't making me any money. Would blocking off this time mean pouring more energy into an ongoing failure? Well, I thought, it would be if I never finished.

As we committed to specific writing times and set goals for what we intended to accomplish that week, I got to know more about my classmates' projects. George, a retired tech guy, an anarchist in black jeans and a black T-shirt, had taken his novel apart piece by piece, as if he were dismantling a watch. His problem was not plot, he said; it was emotions. He had embarked on a serious reconsideration of each character's emotional development, starting with the subordinate characters. He was almost finished with those and, by the end of the month, wanted to start doing the same for the major ones. I found his meticulous process fascinating, particularly when he unfurled the outline of his three-hundred-page book: five eight-and-a-half-by-fourteen-inch sheets of paper taped together, which he spread out on the floor of Cary's living room and then folded up neatly and tucked back into the proper place in his black knapsack.

Fay, a Malaysian graduate of MIT, came to Finishing School a refugee from a brutal writing class. Fay had tired of the teacher who wanted to talk about process all the time. The class became about whether or not you had followed his process exactly as he had described. She sought out Finishing School because she wanted something more open, less directed.

She started to describe her screenplay in bold strokes but quickly shifted to describing a community-planning process that she was organizing in her North Beach neighborhood. Her degree at MIT had been in urban planning, and in this experiment she was using several inventive techniques to get everyone in the neighborhood, people of all races and all ages, to participate in the process rather than just arguing the fine points of the plan the city had devised. She sat up sharply, her back no longer resting in the chair, and her hands moved freely in the air as she described the found objects she'd collected to stimulate discussion in these sessions.

Fay decided that in this month of Finishing School she would work on the protagonist in her screenplay because she thought some of that character's actions didn't line up consistently. She believed if she could get this right, she'd be able to finish the draft quickly. "You seem a lot more excited talking about that planning experiment," Cary observed. "Maybe you should write about that." Fay said she'd come to work on her screenplay and she was committed to it.

Christina, with long dark hair, sharp glasses, and a deep, droll voice, was a returning student. Earlier in the year she'd taken Finishing School for a month, and in three weeks she had finished a script she had been struggling with for more than a year. She writes comedy and she spoke rapidly with a dry sense of humor when she described her new project, a memoir of the two years she'd spent in the same writing class that her friend Fay had fled.

That writing class met for two hours a week online, in a format where all class members were visible in thumbnail on the periphery of the screen while the teacher held forth in a larger square at the center. His specialty was conflict. He taught that stories that didn't have a valid conflict at the center were weak and had clumsy endings. He was all about conflict in real life too. He would go off on a student's work, quoting passages he hated in the student's writing, attacking them for poor craft and sloppy work habits. In looking at the script she'd been working on at the time, Christina saw the wisdom of this advice. Conflict is the essence of drama, the way the writer moves things forward and also reveals character through moments when people clash or face obstacles that prevent them from getting what they want. Without conflicts, the characters are just being drawn along through their lives without incident, and the audience begins to lose interest.

When Christina took the teacher's advice and put more conflict in her scripts, she started having more conflict in her life. She began to examine the places where she chose to engage in a conflict and those where she did not. Even though she found many aspects of her life irritating, Christina realized she rarely voiced her strong opinions. People around her didn't often know what she was thinking. After experiencing the power of conflict to move a screenplay plot forward, Christina became impatient with the plot of her life. She found the courage to speak up to some friends who had been taking advantage of her. Then Christina raised some big issues that had been bothering her in her relationship and subsequently dropped her boyfriend. Finally she acted on her dissatisfaction with her job. Her whole life became turmoil, which, considering Christina's dry wit, provided the basis for a funny memoir. At the first meeting of the month of Finishing School, she had twenty-five thousand words of her memoir. Her goal was to get to forty thousand by the end of the month.

My turn. I described my book proposal about the secret world of trains. I explained that my daughter traveled the rails for a year and a half, a time of great worry for me. In pursuing her, I had discovered a whole secret world that operates in the shadows between the mile-long freight trains. I had developed a wide number of sources, many of them prisoners who had been convicted of crimes on the rails. I had a huge file of correspondence with them. The assignment I gave myself for the week ahead was to reread all those letters and, as I already had a structure I liked for the proposal, write extended summaries of all of the chapters for the proposal outline.

Cary's goal for the month was to decide on a title and the pitch for a novel he'd been working on for many years. After we set our goals, we put our names into a hat and drew partners. I got Christina. We pledged to text each other when we began to write and when we stopped. As Cary drew back the curtain, signaling the end of class, I saw, under the dome of a glass cake pedestal on the kitchen counter, a platter of dark chocolate brownies still warm from the oven. Norma, Cary's wife, is an accomplished cook who after class offered up a baked good— spice cake, cookies, a dense chocolate tart—and a block of cheese and some crackers, to encourage students to linger. It worked.

My first scheduled writing time wasn't for a few days, but Christina started right away. When my phone pinged, announcing a new text, I was pleased to see it was from Christina. "Starting now." The thought of her sitting down at her desk made me smile. Go get 'em, Christina. I'll be there with you on Thursday.

At my appointed time, I texted Christina. Then I gathered

up all the letters from my prison sources and put them in sequence. When I opened the first one and started to read, it was as if I were reading it for the first time. In all the hours I had spent in torment, part of my insecurity was the feeling that I didn't have enough information to write this proposal, let alone this book. As I read the letters, it became clear that while I had to do a lot more reporting, what I had was astonishingly candid and very rich in detail. After just one two-hour session, I was excited by this project again. I was sad when my timer went off and I had to stop. I texted Christina about my insight. She was encouraging in her reply. "That's great. You'll do even better tomorrow."

The second week everyone had made great progress. George, in his measured way, was steadily on track. Christina had written more than three thousand words. Fay was the most remarkable of all. In her first block of writing time, she'd looked at her protagonist and decided that she had been trying to cram too much into one movie. She realized that Cary was right. She was straining when she talked about her screenplay. What she really wanted to write about was the planning experiment. For the rest of Finishing School, she decided, she would write two articles on city planning and try to get them published. Her face was open and joyful as she described how she would tackle this new goal.

After that second session, when the habits of Finishing School were better embedded in my schedule, I suggested to a writer friend that perhaps it might be useful for him to enroll. He had had many early successes but hadn't published much in the last twenty years. He balked at being in a group of any kind, particularly a group of other writers. "I can't be in writing groups," he said. "I don't like to read amateur writers' work. It's hard for me to be polite about bad writing."

I agreed with him. He'd described one of the reasons that I'd been very uncomfortable in both of the previous writing groups I'd briefly attended. Sometimes the writing the other students turned in was so poor I did not have anything helpful to say, which made me feel bad. I didn't want to be brutally honest and crush them, but I also felt as though I were betraying the group spirit by not advising them. In Finishing School we do not read each other's work, which allows us to meet as equals. Those who have been published, and those who are yet to be, share common struggles in trying to finish their work. Reading each other's work stands in the way of this egalitarian ideal. Sure some of us are more talented than others, and some of us are further along in the work, but by focusing solely on what gets in the way of working we support each other regardless of that day's or that week's product. Finishing School helps us to drop all the "writer" nonsense that has us jockeying for a place in the hierarchy and to see ourselves as craftspeople who work with the tools we have at hand.

Then Cary shared his ongoing efforts to finish his novel. His novel started as a short story that was published in a Canadian literary journal in 1995. In the last twenty years, Cary has had plenty of long stretches when he worked well, but two decades after the story was published he realized that he had no plan or timetable for completing the work.

When Cary started on the novel, it was 1995, his freelance career had stalled, and he had taken a job as a copy editor working on industrial-safety manuals for an oil company. He had gone from waking when he chose and starting the day at a café to leaving the house at 7:00 a.m., wearing a tie, with gel raked through his thin, sandy-brown hair. He had his favorite seat on the streetcar, the jump seat at the articulation point where the car bends. If anyone else snagged that seat, he'd be in a bad mood all morning. This costume and these fussy pleasures were signs of his mounting misery, which disappeared once he decided to use the forty-five-minute streetcar ride to work on the novel.

That decision took the edge off his professional collapse. Every day he was first in line when the streetcar door opened, eager to grab the jump seat and take out his notebook. As he wrote freely, the story unfolded in a California delta town, with fully realized scenes and characters with complex backstories. During that hour and a half each day that he wrote on the streetcar, he was optimistic. The novel would be his route out of his drudgery.

In 1999 the online publication *Salon* hired Cary, and he set the novel aside when he began his daily advice column. From time to time he'd pick up the novel again, but he'd drop it quickly, because while there was a lot of good material, he no longer knew what the novel was about. When asked for a title or a plot synopsis, he came up blank. He described those feelings as "I want to cringe. I want to curl into a ball. My life is draining away because I keep doing the wrong things."

The gnawing problem of his unfinished novel was the motivation for Finishing School. The novel had become a shameful secret from which he needed relief. Although he had had plenty of success as a writer, the unfinished novel swallowed that up, leaving him with only the identity of failure. He knew that when you shared your secret with others you felt less ashamed. In the tradition of Alcoholics Anonymous, Cary wanted a place where he could stand in front of others and say aloud, "I'm Cary Tennis and I'm in deep shit with my novel." He started Finishing School in February 2013, with the personal goal of using his time there to shape the hundred thousand words he'd written. He needed to make some basic decisions, such as: Who was the main character? What was the plot?

These seem like simple questions, but they are crucial ones that Cary had never clearly answered as he wrote with abandon on the jump seat. Through Finishing School, he has answered these questions. I took a lot of joy from watching Cary decide on the main character, identify the central conflict, and pick a catchy title for his work. I saw how George, who also had an unwieldy, long-neglected project he was trying to revive, was boosted by Cary's remarkable progress in just the two months we were in class together.

One of the benefits of reporting to others in the class about how the week went is that in summing up you remind yourself that you made progress even if you didn't fulfill your goal. I was still banging my head against a wall, unable to figure out what was wrong, but I could also point to success in completing a piece of writing, doing some research, trying to better define a central idea. Too often when a project stalls, I tend to think only of the parts I have yet to solve, rather than the many other positive aspects of the project. The weekly report to my classmates forced me to see the successes alongside the continuing frustrations.

In the final week of the month, the last session is a celebration. For the "throwdown" students bring printouts of what they have completed in the month of Finishing School. When it's your turn, you slam the completed pages down on the floor and enjoy the thud they make. Everyone applauds.

During that last session of the month, Fay was beaming. She'd not only decided something important about her screenplay, she'd written two articles and come up with an idea for a film festival, which that week she had started organizing. George had met his goal, and Christina had completed a first draft of her memoir. She would be leaving Finishing School after this session but swore she'd be back in a few months. Cary had settled on the title and the pitch for his novel.

I threw down my first draft of the proposal, a big moment for me even though I knew it needed another draft. Between the third and fourth weeks, I'd understood what was holding me back. To tell this story, I had to write about a difficult time with my daughter. I needed to think hard about this and talk to my daughter about it, so I agreed to spend another month in Finishing School, to keep on track during the month of November. I fully expected to have a completed second draft at the end of the next month, and I was pleased to know that George and Fay were continuing as well.

After I completed the second draft of my proposal in November, I asked Cary if he'd be open to writing a book about Finishing School. I was impressed that this simple, easily reproducible method was just as effective for professional writers as it was for beginners. When he said yes, I interviewed the other students to get a sense of how Finishing School had helped them and why they kept coming back.

Despite how disciplined and deliberate George appeared, he said he signed up for Finishing School to help with his procrastination. He'd had a hard time maintaining hope about a project that had been going on for so many years. "I felt like the novel was incomplete, but at the same time I didn't have the motivation to carry it through on my own. There was something about sitting in front of my own computer, staring at that screen; it just wasn't coming. On my thirteenth rewrite, no one was telling me that this needed to get done this year or the following year. I had some magical thinking going on. 'I'll take care of it. I'll get to it.' That magic never came through. Finishing School gave me a fake deadline, but there I was in a group of people rooting for me, and if I said to them, 'Oh, I fucked off,' I wouldn't feel very good about myself."

Although Fay was not a procrastinator, she had trouble seeing herself as a writer, and this ended up getting in the way of doing the work. "In Finishing School I came into being a writer, the personality and the habits of being a writer. It gave me a place where I validated the writer in me, and that let me take chances. I've been in a lot of other writing groups and I was never that prolific. Here I birthed the film festival. I wrote two articles. When I turned in the first article to a magazine, I was thrilled that they referred to me as 'the writer.' Most of the time I'm a banker or a mother, but the foundation of my identity is as a writer, and Finishing School brought that to me."

Christina seemed to be so productive that she wouldn't need Finishing School. Turns out she found that productivity thanks to Finishing School. In the conflict-ridden writing class, she chafed against what she called "the scarcity model" of writers' groups. "Only one of you is going to make it. Is it going to be you?" her previous teacher had said.

"Cary wants all of us to succeed," Christina noted. "Finishing

School is like a lifeline to me. I had been doing *The Artist's Way* program, and I was writing, but I wasn't finishing things. You start, you accumulate material, start great things, but how do you finish them? How do we complete things? How do we say that we're done? *The Artist's Way* gets you started. Finishing School gets you finished."

Cary also teaches an online version of Finishing School, which he allowed me to observe. The writers there had similar successes as those in the class I attended at Cary's house. In the first session I observed, Tanya, who was working on her long-neglected PhD dissertation, said simply, "I've done a lot more this week than I've done in a long time. I do my best work when I can break it down. Like today I'm working on this little subsection of a chapter. That's perfect for me."

April was most pleased with the arrival of a creative buddy in her life. "I can make this into such punishment and drive myself crazy. All of that is gone. This buddy system is terrific," she said. "The buddy is not here to meet our unconscious needs. No judgment about how far, how fast, how good. This is not a competition. We're both just running the race."

Craig, who had been working on a novel for five years, was inspired by his new buddy. "Encouraging her encourages me. I wrote to her after I'd worked ten to midnight. That's what's happened because I feel responsible to her. I'm sitting down for at least an hour every night, spreading out my old notes and putting names on them. Just remember, five minutes of doing is better than thirty minutes of 'meant to do.' You can make a huge breakthrough in five minutes. Having someone waiting for you is huge. Without having someone to report to, the week slips away. Oh, I'll do it tomorrow, tomorrow, tomorrow."

Craig was so energized that when he had to bring the family car in for service at the dealership, he brought a notebook with him and spent the hours there "working on getting the story straight and not worrying about what will go on the printed page." He was so consumed with this work that he was surprised, and a little disappointed, when the mechanic told him the car was ready. "Having it in your head is one thing. Putting it down on the page is another," he said. "This is no longer potential or dream or anything like that. It's getting done."

The person I felt the most inspired by was Ellen, who was working on a collection of short stories but hadn't touched them in years. Ellen confessed that she was a hoarder. The room she had always envisioned as her place to write was so crammed with stuff that she could barely open the door. The task she brought into her month of Finishing School was not writing per se but clearing out that room.

The job seemed herculean, and all of us appreciated how the cycle of failure began in the inaccessibility of that room, as if the writer in her were buried under all that clutter. How frustrating it must have been for Ellen to have the desire to write but no place to do it. Of all the tasks Ellen was responsible for in life, cleaning out that room was right next to dental surgery in its lack of appeal. Yet steadily, week by week, through Finishing School, Ellen cleaned out the room, cleared off a table, and arranged the paper and other tools she needed to write. Everyone in the class was overjoyed by her victory. She pledged to continue another month in Finishing School, a month when she would start to write.

Ellen's struggle revealed to me how many seemingly unrelated tasks a writer has to complete before he or she can finish.

All that time spent in self-abuse, like my punishing monologues as I drove to my unsuccessful writing retreats, weigh down the creative impulse, mire the writer in doubt, and make the whole enterprise seem futile. The busyness and the pressures of the world are designed to discourage creativity and enforce the numbing regularity of everyday life, conformity, and acquiescence. As Cary said when he was signing off on the last session of that month of online Finishing School, "During this whole process of developing Finishing School, I've had to confront my patterns of finishing and not finishing. Don't you want your work out there? Don't you want to get it in a magazine? Those of us who are creative, it's our job to stir things up."

My two months in Finishing School certainly stirred me up by revealing the obstacles I had thrown in my path. When my project was going poorly, I thought about it and myself with such bruising negativity that those thoughts had a powerful impact on me. I believed that enduring this brutality was a form of working on my book, when it definitely was not.

The question at the heart of Finishing School is: did you write when you said you would? Finishing School first got me to stop lying to myself by teaching me that work was writing, not self-abuse monologues.

The first of the Six Emotional Pitfalls that stood in the way of completing my project was arrogance. I felt very uncomfortable admitting that I needed help. At first I mouthed the right words about us all being peers, but secretly I was a bit smug about my professional success and how that set me apart from others. This was on my mind when I drove to Finishing School for the first class. However, I repressed my arrogance when I met the other students, all of whom were very sincere about their goals, plus fun, witty, and smart.

Still, my arrogance arose when we identified our goals for the week. Mine were remarkably overambitious, much grander than I would have chosen for one of the ghostwriting projects, where my estimates of what I can do in an hour or in a week are accurate.

In the first meeting I pledged to write all the summaries for the sixteen chapters of the book proposal *and* read the letters from my source in prison. I had a bit of an attitude. I thought, "I'll show these people how it's done." I bragged that I was going to complete so much work in the six hours I had allotted to the project that week. The great thing about failing within the context of Finishing School is that when you describe your week and what went well and what went poorly, you release the bad feeling that comes with the failure. In my case, I was able also to make fun of myself for my absurd goals. When you work on your own and you get to the end of another week having accomplished nothing, you feel terrible. Here I did one part of what I had pledged to do—reading the letters—and I felt great about myself and the project. It was moving forward for the first time in a long while. Plus I learned about my arrogance.

As I read the letters, it became clear that I'd also surrendered progress in my work to the idea that I had more research to do. I was in the middle of "I'll never know enough." Instead of recognizing the strength of what I had, I focused on what I didn't have. I was surprised at how quickly that pitfall disappeared in my first work session, and grateful too.

Next I fell into the judgment trap—"I'm willing to be judged, but only if I'm judged the victor." I feared that I couldn't measure up to my own expectations. I had written books for and with famous people, never one under my name alone. I had endured some humiliations in the course of my fifteen years as a ghostwriter and often fell into despair that my talents would never be celebrated in the way I thought they should. My book had to be great to repay me for all that suffering. I couldn't be satisfied unless my book was an instant classic, talked about in the press and widely reviewed. But, I thought, I was a bad writer or I would have written my own book years ago. Ghostwriting had tarnished my talents and I was not skilled enough to pull it off. The yearning for perfection, and even redemption, through writing had stopped me. What if it was ignored? Fear of being judged and fear of not being judged! And despite how I had poohpoohed amateur writers' precious fountain pens and Moleskine notebooks, I recognized through Finishing School that I had arranged for my own much more elaborate symbolic victories in making my pilgrimage to Nyack and taking those weekends in the cabin in the redwoods.

The more I thought about it, the harder it was to disentangle the pitfalls from each other. Fear, judgment, and shame always seem to travel together; doubt and fear are rarely apart. Writer's block is a bulky heap of insecurities and phobias. In my arrogance and isolation, I thought these stalling tactics and panicked moments were unique to my shameful failures as a writer, but in the two months I spent among the other working writers in Finishing School we all shared these. Finishing School kept me on track despite it all.

The Problem with Writers' Groups and How Finishing School Is Different

Danelle

PEOPLE JOIN WRITERS' groups for many reasons. They may believe that joining one will compel them to write regularly. Writing can be lonely, so it's natural to seek out an audience of keen listeners to help you get a sense of whether anyone understands what you're trying to say. After you've worked a piece of writing over and over, doubted it, rewritten it, even discarded it, you may lose the ability to judge it. Is it brilliant or is it embarrassing? Perhaps if you found other writers to hear your work, you'd get a better sense of what to do next. Also, writers often hope to receive a professional critique from the leader of the group.

These are all good, sensible reasons. What many do not realize is that they also come to the writers' group with unstated or unconscious needs: looking for love, acceptance, recognition, fame, and to find other writers who will help them get published. Writers' groups are usually not equipped to fill those hidden needs. For this reason, people sometimes get their hearts broken in writers' groups. They come away thinking not that they were in a bad writers' group but *that they are bad writers.*

Finishing School avoids this danger. Since we do not share work, there are no stars, no prima donnas, no hopelessly untalented wannabes. We come together as equals, dedicated only to making progress in our projects, whether they be quixotic and ill conceived or utterly brilliant. The freedom and confidence this discipline confers on an individual is remarkable. You are responsible for your own work. We applaud you in the doing of it. We ask writers to do something very simple: set clear goals supported by well-defined tasks. For many writers, this is entirely new. They have always written intuitively, as if by magic, heading into the forest to wander and discover what is there, without regard for a destination or an outcome. For Cary, in particular, this was revolutionary. Stating out loud what he hoped to accomplish in his work on the novel was at first frightening. He had worked in secret, protecting his work from all scrutiny, as if any scrutiny might damage the work or skew his highly personal vision.

We're not shaming people who join writers' groups. We don't look down on them. We've both been members of writers' groups, and Cary now leads them, although his groups strictly follow the ethical guidelines of the Amherst Writers and Artists method. We admire the courage it takes to join a writers' group. We just think that certain practices in certain groups are dangerous and foolhardy, and we want to save people from the consequences.

We understand the tender state the writer is in when he or she tries to find an audience that will be truthful, helpful, and kind. Most of us spend a lot of energy in protecting our private lives and run as fast as we can from places where we will be judged. Yet as writers we invite scrutiny. First drafts are flawed attempts at expression and thus a place of vulnerability. What keeps you going as a writer is that yearning for perfection, but what you offer up with a shaky hand to a roomful of strangers is your much-less-than-perfect self. You present this malformed, belabored, sometimes half-assed piece of work to a bunch of people who have agendas of their own. You also are likely to face the Six Emotional Pitfalls—doubt, fear, shame, arrogance, yearning, judgment—in the faces of people just a few inches from your own. This can reinforce, rather than release you from, the patterns that keep you from finishing.

Moreover, when people come to a group with wildly different levels of skill and commitment, suddenly the group self-sorts into cool people and not-so-cool people. Often someone who is good at critique becomes the leader of the group; a good critic isn't necessarily a good teacher. He or she is likely to inhibit your inner creative voice rather than inspire you to write more. Another member may wow the group with a perfect chapter, creating envy and unearthing insecurities the others didn't even know they had. What was meant to clear the skies overhead instead darkens them with interpersonal politics and jealousy. We've seen that writers' groups often start off strong, but by the six-month mark the numbers have thinned considerably.

There are certainly exceptions. There are rare writers' groups that go on for years, in which members express their opinions in a compassionate manner and try to focus on the good in the other members' work. But even in the best of writers' groups the goal is rarely finishing but, rather, perfecting.

This can be a trap that sends you rewriting before it is useful—and prevents that first draft or second draft from ever being realized.

Don't get trapped among the energy vampires. Here are two questions to ask yourself to determine if your writing group is causing you harm. They have to do with what happens to you after you leave the meeting. After your writers' group meets, do you feel like writing? If you don't, then you're in a group that is not good for you. Also, after meeting, do you find yourself rehearsing speeches to other members of the group, mulling over responses you wish you'd been quick enough to come up with when you felt cornered by a comment one of the other members made? That means the status sorting and politics of the group have overtaken the real reasons that you joined.

Finishing School is not like these writing groups because it's not about the worth of the work; it's about the working. We leave it up to you to judge if the writing is good or bad and if there is more to be done to finish. If you are working consistently, you know when it is going well and you know when it is not. If the writing is not going well, your fellow Finishing School members can help you find tactics that work. They may advise you not to expect to finish this scene or finish this chapter this week. Maybe you need to do a diagnostic. Reread the material with an eye toward the bigger idea of what's wrong with it, not the details. So you commit to sit for two hours and think, or maybe go paragraph by paragraph. Perhaps you're not going to fix these things during that next week, but you are going to honestly address the problem. These reflective times are not impediments but, rather, crucial steps toward finishing.

What Can You Accomplish in One Month?

Cary

I THINK YOU will be surprised at how much you can accomplish in one month once you begin using Finishing School.

How do we do it?

At our first meeting, we ask a simple question: what do you want to get done this month?

In a typical month you have about thirty days multiplied by sixteen waking hours per day, or about four hundred eighty hours of waking consciousness, to do all the things you do. How many of those four hundred eighty hours might be available for you to work on the most important project in your life? Three? Five? Seven? Twenty-four? Maybe more?

I say "the most important project in your life" because for this one month it has that privilege. Ceding to this work that honored position is part of the trick of Finishing School.

Get out your calendar. Look at the month. Look at all those days. What are those days filled with? Is there room in there somewhere for the most important thing in your life? Try penciling in some times. Look at periods where you don't specifically know what you're doing. Maybe that time is spent in unstructured and somewhat chaotic ways. Maybe it is in unthinking service or "availability" to others. Whose time is this anyway? It is your time, for heaven's sake! You were put on this earth and slotted an unknown but certainly finite number of hours, and those are your hours on this earth. As long as you are not behind bars, and even if you are behind bars, you have this time and you can choose how to use it. So take some of it. Demarcate it. Mark it off on your calendar. Declare it as yours. Schedule it. You don't have to tell anyone how you are using that time. Just call it "appointments" or "meetings" or "things." Just say, "Oh, tomorrow I can't. I have a thing from two to four."

"What thing?"

"Oh, it's just this thing I do. I can't get out of it."

It's your frigging time. Take it.

IT HELPS TO use metaphors. Try building fences around your time. Maybe your family and friends consider you always "available." Try earmarking some of that time for this project and announcing to family and friends that you are not available: "Between the hours of one and four on Thursdays, I'm not available."

Find a place where you can shut the door. Or leave the house and don't take your cell phone. Park your car on a bluff and write. Go to McDonald's and write. Take a walk and talk into your audio recorder. Ask a friend if you can use a room in their place. Go into your office during nonwork hours. Say you are going to bed and then instead sit up in bed and write. Go up on the roof. Sit in the garage. Find a tree. There are many ways to escape. And escape is necessary. Taking time for creative work in certain ways requires escape—there are no two ways about it—because our daily lives are designed to keep us away from solitary voluntary work. I don't know how it worked out to be that way, but it is that way. We are subject to innumerable authorities—work, school, family, friends. We must rebel, either openly or furtively. So get in touch with your spirit of rebellion. Take pleasure in defeating the enemy. It is for a good cause.

NEXT, AT A typical first meeting of Finishing School we ask, what are the components of this thing you want to get done this month? This usually requires some thought on the part of the creative artist who has shown up. What are the components? Good question. Just considering them as components can take you a long way toward mastery of the project. They are just components. As they are completed, one by one, you will approach completion of the project.

Along with this we ask, how long will each component take? Chances are, at first you will not know. You may not have broken it down this way before. Maybe your method is just to go into your workspace and start working until you are too tired or have to go somewhere to pick up the kids. Then we ask, how much time do you have to devote to these components? We break it down into weeks. Okay, this thing you want to get done this month, what would one-quarter of it look like?

This is an amazing thing. Sometimes it is very hard. Sometimes it is a revelation. For instance, I may think, okay, I would like to get six chapters done this month. Well, how long does each chapter usually take you?

I don't know! I never thought about it before.

Well, okay. So now we are thinking about it. Let's find out.

That is the beauty of Finishing School. By breaking time into manageable pieces, and breaking our projects into manageable pieces, we discover what we are doing. It feels like a new form of reality.

The Four Phases
of Creativity

Cary

IN 1926 THE English socialist thinker Graham Wallas published *The Art of Thought*, in which he proposed four general phases of creative activity: preparation, incubation, illumination, and verification. Many variations of this idea have been proposed since then (just Google "phases of creativity"), but in Finishing School we think Wallas's fourfold scheme is a great road map to look at when you're lost. No matter how complicated your project seems to be, you can always step back and ask, "Okay, given that there are four phases of creativity, what phase am I in, and what does that tell me about the tasks I need to be performing?"

Phase 1: Preparation
Investigate and define the issue.

Phase 2: Incubation
Let the ideas simmer.

Phase 3: Illumination

Aha! The ideas come together.

Phase 4: Verification

Look at your output in the harsh light of day.

Say you are shuffling papers and rereading text files. You don't seem to be getting anywhere. You wonder, "Is this productive work or just avoidance?" If you look at the four phases, you may realize that you are in the preparation phase. Then you can regard your work as bona fide preparation.

Knowing that you are in the preparation phase, you can ask some pertinent questions: What concrete thing do I need to accomplish or prepare for? What documents are important to my project? What am I looking for in this mass of papers? You can make yourself a little list of things you need to do. That can then become your concrete set of goals for the week. You come to Finishing School and you say, "I think I am in the preparation phase this week, and so I am going to use my time to put all these things in a notebook, or arrange them in chronological order, or pick the best, most promising ones and set about polishing them, or put everything into Scrivener." Good. You've made some progress. You can feel good about that.

OR PERHAPS YOU are in a different phase. You feel utterly becalmed, distant from your project. You're doing nothing. Are you stuck? Maybe. You could try sitting with the project and see if something comes. But if not, perhaps you are in the incubation phase. Your future creation is being prepared for you outside of conscious awareness. Relax. Know that this is so. It will come. Wait for it. Do something else. Do not panic. Maintain an open, receptive, welcoming attitude toward this work. Know that it will come. This would be an excellent time to go buy office supplies. The image comes to mind of how expectant mothers buy blankets and things for the baby. They know it's coming. So they prepare.

Then one day this happens: without any plan or preconceived notion, you are swept away in a wave of productivity! This is amazing! It should always be like this! You cancel appointments and ignore your family. The illumination phase might last only an afternoon, or it might last for days. You might eat sporadically at your desk or wander alone, your head filled with thoughts and voices. You might scribble on notepads while shopping or not even go shopping but sit at home and eat leftovers and make sandwiches. You might forget to bathe and ignore appointments. This thing has come and taken over and changed your life. You are an artist! This is what it's like!

Then it slows down. You wake up one morning full of worries, with a distracted mind and no thought of anything creative or beautiful. "Wow, what was that?" you wonder. "I'd like some more of that! How did that happen? Where did it go? Why isn't work always like that?"

This too is a part of the phase of illumination. You may feel exhausted or even depressed after such an experience. If you do not honor it as another of the necessary, inevitable phases of the creative cycle, you may try all sorts of methods to stay in. How can I keep this avalanche of creativity going? How? You may be tempted to take stimulants or mind-altering drugs to keep it going. You may feel desperately disappointed.

But it has not dumped you in the desert. It has just led you to the next necessary phase, which Wallas calls verification. So you have just painted up a storm, or designed a new city, or written fifty thousand words. Now what? Verification is the "now what?" phase. Having produced all this material, we ask: Now what? What do we do now with this huge pile of words? It is time to reenter the world, connect with others, confess what has happened, and make a plan. Perhaps at this point you call in an editor or other outside help. Verification involves a new set of eyes, be they yours or someone else's. It may involve submission: see what editors of journals think. Maybe there is something brilliant in there and you can't see it yet, or maybe it is a beginning whose implications you cannot yet appreciate.

ONCE I THOUGHT about the phases of creativity, I saw that the reason we call them phases is that they are separate! They have to be regarded separately. You can't do them all at the same time. You can't simultaneously prepare and illuminate. You can't simultaneously illuminate and verify. That's the whole point of knowing there are phases: so you can know what phase you are in and concentrate on that alone.

In many ways, the preparation phase is the most daunting. You prepare yourself and get together what you need. What do you need?

That requires you to know what you are trying to make.

Here comes a paradox: in looking at all the material you created supposedly for the novel, you may see that the very existence of all this material makes it hard to see the novel itself.

So begin some thought experiments. Take a piece you have

written and ask: Is this the core of the novel? Could this be the beginning? What is this piece about? Is this piece about what the novel is about?

Take notice: What answer comes to you quickly? What is your intuitive, immediate response? Is this what the novel is about? Is it what the novel is? Use your gut sense. Does it go in or out? You don't have to throw it away. You can just put it aside. In this initial pass, you are looking for pieces that seem like they are the novel. This can be an intuitive judgment, a hunch. Artworks achieve luminescence by repetition of components, each of which in some way also contains the whole, so that there is a harmony and echoing in the work, but this takes place below the viewer's threshold of consciousness. So if a piece seems like it belongs, it very well may. You must learn to trust your instincts in this matter. The artist must decide which pieces contain the whole of the vision or are essential to the vision. That is how you decide what to do with all this material. That is preparation. You schedule time for it in Finishing School. You check in with your buddy. You go to where the material is. You sit with it. You look at the pieces but you limit the activities you will engage in—i.e., no writing or editing, just choosing of pieces!

RECOGNIZING THESE PHASES helps you give yourself over to the process of creativity without undue anxiety and worry. That is the benefit of knowing what phase you are in: You can more completely give yourself over to the task at hand. You can let go of doubt and fear, and simply sort papers or catalog negatives if you are in the preparation phase; or write with abandon, not editing as you go, if you are in the illumination phase; or calmly and carefully go over your work, examining it for flaws and inconsistencies and making little improvements, if you are in the verification phase; or just hang around the house, moping or shooting baskets or reading the paper or taking a bath, if you are in the incubation phase.

There is nothing profound we need to know about these phases. Nothing we can learn about them will help us "do" them any better. It is more a matter of opening your eyes and seeing where you are.

On Not Reading Each Other's Work

Danelle

STUDENTS COME TO writing groups expecting that the people they meet there will read their work and react to it with helpful advice. In Finishing School we do not read each other's work and we do not offer feedback. There is a specific reason for this. We think random feedback, from people you do not know well and on a piece that may not yet be ready, is often destructive. We want Finishing School to be a place that is completely supportive of your writing and the complex task of trying to finish, no matter who you are and how much or how little writing you have done before you come to class.

When you send your chapter off to the writers' group, you fall instantly into the pitfalls. Yearning for perfection and for acclaim. Doubt that it is good enough. Shame that the fact that it is not good enough reflects poorly on you. Fear of being judged often comes with flashes of arrogance during which you convince yourself that the others are idiots who have no right to judge. This delays progress on your work between the time you have sent your sample and the day of the class. You may spin your wheels, frantically revising the piece, even after you sent it, although the other members of your group will never see the newer drafts. This is writing busy work, nervous motion. Recovering from the class may take some time too. With all the voices in your head and the contradictory advice, you may not know what you should do next. And you may fall into despair and think the task before you is impossible.

In Finishing School we trust that you know what you are doing and will reveal your work to someone you have chosen carefully, at a moment when you need guidance. The issue we tackle is not the quality of the work on any given Tuesday but the habit of writing. We want to take the drama out of your identity as a writer so you can spend that energy in writing. We all know writing is hard and that there will be days of glory amid the long commitment to the work. Finishing School's sole focus is the steady application of time to the craft, every week reinforcing the qualities and habits necessary to one day saying that you are done. You are on no one's timetable but your own. Your steady attendance at Finishing School demonstrates a serious commitment to the task, which is all that is required.

This makes Finishing School egalitarian. Both beginning and accomplished writers can sit comfortably beside more successful ones, supporting one another in reaching the goal. This is why we pick our creative buddies by tossing slips of paper with our names and cell phone numbers on them into a hat. It reinforces the fact that this is something any two people can do together. By not reading each other's work, we minimize negative energy. We're not competing for praise or showing off. We're all there to just deal with this glorious, vexing, maddening problem, and there's a lot more shared pain and celebration of breakthroughs, and a lot less ego, than in a critique group.

The question of personal chemistry between buddies is one that people ask us about, wondering what happens to the process if two people are not suited to be creative buddies or if one is cruel or impatient to their partner. We believe any two people can be creative buddies, because they're not becoming friends. They're just checking in. Chemistry doesn't matter. What matters is just checking in with somebody. But there do seem to be certain combinations where people really hit it off and end up writing together in a café outside of class and reading each other's work. It's complex and not something we can manage. So our emphasis is on the method.

In a purely supportive atmosphere, Finishing School drags you out of the pitfalls so you can get your mind back on the task at hand. If you have decided you are ready to seek feedback on your work, this might be the task you would like to take on for that month of Finishing School. You could discuss in class what you need to do to get your work ready to be read. Your classmates would listen as you describe the handful of people you want to send it to and the reasons why each one of them would be a good audience Likely, just sharing your thoughts with them would help you pare down that list and set objectives for what you want to learn from these responses.

Sending your work off can be an emotional experience, and the group can help you move through that and through the period of waiting for a response. Once you receive feedback, the group is a place where you can air it, get others' opinions about a comment that troubled you. When all of that is complete, the group can help you choose how you want to revise your work, based on this feedback, or if you want to ignore it and plunge on.

I describe this because it highlights how much more support for your writing is available in a Finishing School group. It really does not matter who is in the group with you or their level of insight into your work or whether or not you enjoy theirs. As the relationship is one purely of support, there has never been in our experience a member of the group who was dismissive or condescending when giving or receiving support. If we were more intertwined and commenting on each other's work, judging each other, that might arise, but the conditions are organized so that it's pretty difficult to do unless you are aggressive and judgmental. People like that will not find Finishing School a good solution to their problems.

Part 3

Dealing with
Time Itself

Time and Its Tricks

Cary

WHEN I WAS a child, things that were scheduled did not happen. My father would say we'd go fishing next week, so I would get excited about going fishing. But often as not, something would come up or he would forget, and the fishing trip never happened. I would be hurt. I would hide the hurt. I would go off by myself and be sad.

On the other hand, things that weren't planned seemed to happen all the time, sometimes spectacularly so. We kids would all be taken by surprise when we suddenly discovered we were moving to a new house or giving up meat or making some other unexpected life change. My parents did not gather us together to discuss the future. As far as we were concerned, the future was a vague and possibly bogus notion. That is how I remember my childhood: lots of things talked about and not done, followed by sudden unplanned upheavals.

So perhaps it is not surprising that whenever someone suggests setting a date to do something, in the milliseconds before I am even conscious of my own reaction, I experience a jolt of fear. When I was younger, I thought I could retrain my mind and nervous system, through meditation, to eliminate such responses. Now, at age sixty-two, I do not think I am going to rid myself of these habitual and unconscious responses.

Luckily, I do not have to. All I need to do is follow a program.

Now, I love time. I like to save it and spend it. I can never get enough of time. What I have a problem with is *time management*—I don't like treating time as a resource to be managed. I have a personal relationship with my time. I feel that my time is mine, and I want all of it and do not want to have to manage it as a resource, and I don't want anyone else taking time away from me. I am jealous and protective of my time because I love being in the moment, and when I am in the moment, everything is fine. I could stay here, just like this, and be happy. But then you tell me we have to go now. Something is *scheduled*. You're breaking my heart.

In the past, when I have tried to do time management, I've felt overwhelmed. I was a failure. These feelings have changed over the years as I have gotten better at it. But I do not expect myself to conquer this problem, nor do I want to spend more of my own beautiful time on it.

I just want a system of getting things done so I will not live out a life full of half-finished projects and a head full of regret and sorrow, like my dad.

In my attempts to get better at time management, I have made time maps, as suggested by Julie Morgenstern in her book *Time Management from the Inside Out*. I have also kept detailed daily time and activity logs. Both are useful—the time log shows how your time is actually being spent, and the time map gives you a broad outline with which to group tasks and activities according to their purpose, setting, preferred time of day, etc. Both help to bring order and ease to the slippery, lumpy, unwieldy medium known as time. Keeping a time log, at the very minimum, will increase your awareness of time, making it seem less amorphous and more concrete, and thus more manageable.

Such aids help. And yet I know that unless I am playing music or writing or meditating, or deeply engaged in some activity, I experience time as a terrifying, formless void. Unlike Danelle, I have no knack for scheduling. That's not to say that my relationship to time is totally pathological. There are different personality types, and my personality type—the perceiving type, in Myers-Briggs terminology—prefers to keep possibilities open. That is not all bad. We perceiving types bring to the world an awareness of time's possibilities in the moment. But on the flip side, we don't plan so well. Also, being a creative type as well as a perceiving type, I rely on inspiration for creative work. I do not always know when an idea will arrive, and so my work schedule will sometimes seem chaotic because it is best to work when an idea is most present and vivid.

Can we change our deep-seated nature and habitual preferences? Probably not. But we can take concrete steps to get things done.

For me, the answer is to come together with other people

and say out loud what is going on; sometimes I will have to come to the group and admit that I am not scheduling effectively or not doing what I had planned to do. Once I do that, the burden lifts. It does not seem so awful. I have a chance to make a plan and carry it out.

Yesterday I got completely out of whack with my schedule. This happened because I scheduled things I could not do. I didn't schedule *the possible*. And this, in turn, happened because I did not take the time to think it through. I scheduled under pressure. Now, it's better to schedule poorly, under pressure, than not to schedule at all. Leading a Finishing School workshop in my living room, in which we go around the room recounting the past week's progress and making commitments for the coming week, forced me to schedule. So I scheduled. But I did not schedule wisely or realistically.

I scheduled two hours to work on the novel and two hours to work on writing this book. Tuesday night, I put these items on my calendar for Wednesday. Here they are:

- Work on fifty novel pages, 9–11 a.m.
- Work on *FS* chapter, 1–3 p.m.

What actually happened was that on Wednesday morning I woke up with an idea for writing a pitch, a landing-page sales pitch, for *Finishing School*. I was burning with inspiration for this landing-page sales pitch. So I went straight from bed to work on it. I was excited and the time flew by. I felt like a genius. On this particular Wednesday morning, I felt good about the prospect of writing some sparkling and persuasive advertising copy, so I sailed along doing that instead of what I had scheduled.

Then I looked up, and two hours had gone by. I needed a walk. Wednesday is also the day my column is scheduled to be written, and I had not even put that in my schedule! But it was column-writing day. So I walked down to the café and wrote a column. That too went well.

By then, I had done a lot of writing already. It was difficult to carry out my plan of writing the *Finishing School* chapter and editing the novel. Instead, I remembered other things, business chores, I had to do, so I turned to them with a vengeance. I ended up working until one in the morning.

The next day, after staying up late, I awoke baffled and unhappy because I'd failed to follow my schedule. I had scheduled the impossible. Under pressure, I had just jotted down what I would do without really connecting to it or evaluating it honestly. I did not share with the group that I was actually more interested in these other activities. I was lying to myself and to the group.

I had scheduled without taking into account what I was emotionally and creatively engaged in at the time, nor had I considered my prior commitments. Simply declaring that I would work on these two projects did not change reality. My inner life turned out to be more powerful. My own creativity ruled. My own sense of what was important ruled.

It turns out that I don't do what I tell myself to do, unless I want to.

My relationship with time is still evolving, but I have learned that there are steps I can take to schedule the possible.

Much comes from simple awareness. Making a time map will increase your awareness of time.

Danelle is a master at scheduling the possible. This is something that I observe Danelle doing, and she makes it look easy. One of her tricks is to take stock of what she wants to do and what she does not want to do. But let's let Danelle explain that herself, in the chapter "Writing Day by Day."

Picking Up the Rock
of the Paragraph

Danelle

To FINISH, YOU have to begin. You have to return to that piece of writing that you abandoned some time ago and try to see it with new eyes. Perhaps you had to let it go because life overwhelmed your schedule. You had to deal with an emergency, so you put the writing aside and never picked it up again. Or maybe you started to hate it after a while. You resented the time you were spending on it and began to feel more frustration than anticipation when you thought about your work. Despair sometimes drives people away too, feeling defeated and inadequate. Whatever it was that caused you to stop writing, pledging to finish means that to begin again you will have to set those feelings aside so you can determine how to proceed. This can be difficult. My friend Sarah Kortum has a phrase for this: "picking up the rock of the paragraph."

While Sarah might describe that rock differently, what appealed to me about the rock as a metaphor is the weight of it. We tend to think of our writing as existing in the mind, but if you have done any work, the writing also has a physical manifestation. You may have notebooks or recordings of yourself speaking scenes or dialogue aloud. Perhaps drafts you printed and marked up are stashed in a box high in the closet. These pieces you have touched and now must pick up again are the "rock of the paragraph." They may be small and scattered, but each is just the right size to cradle in your hand. You can pump the rock up and down, and toss it in the air so it settles, heavy in the well of your palm. The paragraph is a solid thing and a place to begin, a building block for the rest of the paragraphs to come. Now, if you can only get yourself to pick it up.

Living with an unfinished novel, enduring the baffling and anguished inability to bring it into workable shape, is a deeply distressing condition for many people. In Finishing School students often arrive at the first meeting a bit shamefaced because they are embarrassed that they do not have a manuscript to polish but a box filled with the kinds of bits and starts described above. Cary has two boxes that contain the pieces of his novel: printouts of drafts, research into important side issues like dry-cleaning methods, San Francisco Muni cars, the Phoenician tin trade, and a time line for all the major characters that stretches back to 5000 BC. Those two file boxes sit in a storage space alongside the many notebooks he filled when he spent his commute writing in the jump seat. All those years of work stuffed into those boxes are proof that his unfinished novel was a physical thing, not just an idea he had one afternoon.

When you think of all the hours, all the craft and the emotions contained in those boxes, it is no wonder that people come to Finishing School seeking guidance on how to begin again. They are having a hard time opening up those boxes. Work left undone for years affects people's moods, their feelings about themselves, their ability to work creatively, and their hopes for the future. We have found, after working on this with many people in Finishing School, that picking up the rock of the paragraph is an emotional experience that needs a space of its own.

In the first year of Finishing School, Cary had a student who wanted to restart the novel she began shortly after she got her MFA in creative writing. The story was strongly formed in her mind, but its physical manifestation consisted of hand-written journal entries, notes jotted on different sizes of paper stashed in a box at home, and bits of writing in various folders and directories in her computer. In the workshop, she decided her first week's task would be scheduling time to assemble the material and to open these boxes. It turned out that opening the boxes and reading the journal entries had an enormous emotional effect on her, almost more than she could bear.

I observed this same reaction in a student in my class. A woman who had been sexually abused as a teenager twenty years earlier had a box of cassette tapes she had made in the months after the rape on which she described her experience. She had carried this box around with her for decades, unwilling to listen to them and unable to throw it away. I suggested that her assignment for the week was just to hold the tapes in her hand, like picking up the rock of the paragraph. Her hands shook when she tried to put one of the cassettes into the tape recorder, she said. When she got the cassette into the recorder, she did not have the will to turn it on. While she berated herself for being too timid to begin, I saw this as big progress.

Writers are wise to be wary of writing they've neglected. It's best to move slowly, like a dog sniffing a rock. When a dog sees something he's not so sure of, he circles it first. He keeps his head low as he sniffs it out, slowly coming closer. We recommend this same caution when getting back to a neglected piece of writing.

The place to start is with the physical, because in touching it, cataloging it, stacking it like cordwood, you are in the first stages of putting it into order. If you have written many scenes, count them. If you have letters, put them in sequential order and bundle them by year. Maybe you have random bits of dialogue. You don't have to read them if that intimidates you. Just make a file and keep adding to it. These are your basic materials from which you can rebuild your work.

When handled, the work starts to lose its power to undo you. You gain a small degree of mastery over it, and the more you can see it as ordered, the firmer the foundation you are building for the new beginning.

My student took a month preparing to listen to the tapes she'd made as a young woman, but that month was important. I encouraged her to write about what she thought she might be too frightened to hear. She wrote about how she had changed since she'd spoken into the tape recorder. Then she allowed herself to listen to two minutes of tape. Just two minutes, so she could get over the difference between her youthful voice and the voice of a woman twenty-five years older. Most people do not like hearing their recorded voice, and this one had a lot more packed into it than just a chat.

If you don't have source material to contend with, you pick up the rock of the paragraph by reading your writing from years before. Proceed with caution there too. We've seen people get derailed by imagining that what they have is in pretty good shape—at least they remember it that way—so they're just going to sit down and knock off another draft. It's an unreasonable goal. Rereading abandoned work can throw you into despair if it is not as good as you expected it to be. One poorly phrased sentence can convince you that all of it is hopeless. A student in my class who hadn't touched her novel in a year and a half tried to get back to it several times, but every time she did, all she saw was terrible writing and holes in the plot. It was grim to hear her describe it, especially in contrast to the bright feeling she'd displayed when she was talking about the novel more generally in the first class.

I advised her to look, when she opened that first chapter, for the things she liked rather than the things she needed to fix. I wanted her to make comments in the margins when there was a good turn of phrase or a word choice that showed some flair. The student had to discipline herself to see the parts of the work that were good. All first drafts need second drafts, but the motivation to go on can't be built on despair.

This had a very positive effect on the student. Not only did she enjoy reading her neglected first chapter, but by the next meeting she had written four thousand words. Her enthusiasm was much stronger and she continued at this pace, adding eight thousand words in the next three weeks.

Cary likes to remind people who are returning to their work about one of the four phases of creativity: preparation. Preparation does not take place on a schedule and should proceed as the material at hand dictates. The material may be telling you to jump right in, as with my student above, or to make slow, deliberate progress, being mindful of your emotions as you encounter the reasons why you gave up on this work you once cared about. The pace does not matter. The important thing is picking up the rock of this paragraph and then the next one after that.

My Fake Schedule

Danelle

THE SCHEDULE EXISTS in an ideal world where there are no distractions or failures of the will that prevent you from meeting these appointments. Some parts of the schedule may be habit, in that you know you get up every morning around the same time and have a day when you go to the grocery store each week and another when you do your laundry. If keeping the appointment on the schedule means someone is going to give you money, or the commitment has to do with health, you are likely to make those appointments. Not so when it comes to writing.

The time you schedule for writing can be fungible. You may have written down that you are going to start at two, but two is when you start making tea, and while making tea, you get caught up in reading something on the phone. The reading on the phone may lead to another thing that interests you, and then another. (Brain Pickings, an Internet site about creativity, can be the most distracting of all, because reading about the brain activity and habits of creative people seems to feel about as good as being creative.) Suddenly you look up and the tea is cold and an hour has passed. When you realize that you've set aside only an hour and a half to write, it may be easy to blow off the remaining half hour by saying that you really cannot get that much done in so little time.

After a series of these minor scheduling defeats, you might think you have to get tough with yourself if you're going to finish this thing. You might sit down with your calendar at the beginning of the week and block off two hours on every weekday and six hours on weekend days. Marking these blocks of time on the calendar can be an extremely satisfying activity. It's as if you were creating an ideal world where you are efficient and dedicated, a model citizen whose extraordinary discipline is proven by the consistent blocks of time you have defined for your creative life. The act of writing down these hours can be so fulfilling, and an escape in a way, that keeping these appointments becomes almost irrelevant. The ecstatic experience of imagining yourself keeping to the schedule for the full week is so satisfying that the actual creative experience often pales by comparison. The schedule becomes the only thing you do that week to support your writing, and it is pretty weak tea.

In truth there are plenty of things that can get in the way of your schedule, particularly when what you are scheduling is something with a long-term payoff, like writing. Writing may be the first thing you are willing to blow off, particularly when it is not going well. Often the people and things in your life require unexpected attention: someone gets sick, a car breaks down, a machine malfunctions, or the dog gets in a fight with another dog and has to go to the veterinarian. When these kinds of events interfere with your schedule, there is little you can do but answer the call of the immediate and put the long-term goal on hold.

Those are not the only forces that will attack the perfection of the fake schedule. There is plain old lack of will. You may know that you are scheduled to start writing at noon on Saturday, but it's pretty comfy on the couch, and there is something inane but amusing on television. Besides, you worked hard all week. Don't you deserve a day off once in a while? And, anyway, you are not so certain that if you sit down to write, something positive will come from it. As soon as noon becomes twelve-thirty, it is easy enough to convince yourself that you've blown it for the day so there is no point in even starting. After all, you'd be starting late.

In the world of the fake schedule, the goals are so extreme that there is not enough spare time to try to reschedule the hours you missed. The week may have begun with a fussy, self-satisfied feeling of perfection, but by the end of the week, when you have kept none, or perhaps just one of the appointments, you end up feeling like a failure no matter what you produced in the hours when you indeed sat down to write.

This is why Finishing School encourages you to be realistic about making a schedule that you can keep. When setting up a schedule for the week, be honest with yourself about how much time you can devote to writing. If it is only an hour, at least you know that you will be able to show up for that hour with something specific to work on that you can finish in that amount of time. The point of making a real schedule is that through keeping your commitment to writing and finishing something each week, you can begin to associate writing with achieving a goal rather than disappointing yourself with your inability to fulfill commitments that are unrealistic for the time you have available. It may seem satisfying to fill out a fake schedule, but at the end of the week it makes you feel like a failure. A real schedule takes into account all the demands life makes on your time and encourages you to write, and to write more.

Setting Achievable Goals
and Meeting Them

Danelle

WHEN MOTIVATIONAL EXPERTS and specialists on time management talk about setting goals, their advice ranges from the mystical to the mechanical, and none of it seems suitable for writers. The mystics advise that all you have to do is set a goal, the bigger the better, and the behaviors and events necessary to accomplish it will fall immediately in line as long as you keep your eyes on that prize. One motivational guru likened goal setting to having an interior GPS: once you've keyed in the destination, the navigational system plots the course and all you have to do is follow the route laid out for you.

The best seller *The Secret* also surrounded goals with mist. *The Secret* promised that if your goal was to find a check for $100,000 in your mailbox, all you had to do was to spend time every day imagining that check, and one day you would open the mailbox and find it there. This life of fantasy goals has a happy palette of pastel colors. It tempts you to experience your goal not as a tangible object at some distance on the horizon, which you are moving toward, but rather as something that rests alongside you on a fluffy cloud.

Many people who come to Finishing School have a terrible relationship with their goals because they live in the world of dreams and not in the tussle of action. At the beginning of each year they set the goal of finishing their book, write the goal down, and never look at it again. Next year they place the same goal in that slot because so little progress has been made. For some, writing down the goal is enough to convince them that they've already accomplished it, much like putting items on a fake schedule. As the years pile up with it unfulfilled, the goal becomes no longer believable. The image *The Secret* credits as so powerful a force for the future becomes proof that the person is fooling around.

Dreaming of your published book makes you feel good in the moment, but it can sap your energy for creative work. Don't assume positive thinking has positive consequences, advises NYU professor Gabriele Oettingen, whose book *Rethinking Positive Thinking* shows that remaining in the dream state prevents you from finishing. In her decades studying long-term motivation and goal setting, she has found that people who had a realistic idea of the obstacles that stood in the way of a cherished goal were more likely to succeed than those who tended a perfect fantasy.

People who spent their time only on positive fantasies were less depressed at the moment, but they got more depressed over time. Oettingen's research showed that when subjects were caught up in these fantasy images they were calmer and happier and their blood pressure lowered a bit. The dreams soothed them and felt like a form of engagement with their vision of the future. These fantasies were a wonderful respite but not a state from which to make an action plan. Imagining this positive outcome was a predictor of lower effort and slower development over time. When she studied students graduating from college and entering the workforce, she found that those with a very positive idea of their postcollege job prospects sent out fewer letters to prospective employers, which meant it took them longer to get a job.

Oettingen's prescription for progress begins with the dream, but dreaming is only part of what gets the job done. Those with a realistic view of the obstacles in the way of accomplishing the task were much more likely to finish. They did not visualize their goal as a finished object way off in the future but saw it as a series of problems that had to be solved to realize it. It is a method that brings up a reckoning with the self, raising the question: how are you getting in the way of your goal?

To FINISH A long piece of writing, you have to complete some practical tasks and some imaginative ones. Both of these skills—the practical and the imaginative—are important to finishing your work. Writers can be anywhere on the continuum between practical and imaginative. If you were to place Cary and me on this axis, Cary would be much more on the imaginative side. My skills are stronger in the realm of the practical, but we each need some of what the other has to finish our work.

With my practical bent, I appreciate business books that give advice about setting goals, which is closer to the Finishing

School method. Many recommend that you set near-term goals, tasks that can be accomplished in a day or a week. When that time period has elapsed, you look at what you've accomplished and move the things that remain to be done to the next week or the next day. I learned this method at *People* magazine when I was assigned to head up the annual weddings issue.

Three months before the May issue featuring the weddings of the stars, we finalized the list of forty celebrity couples who had had lavish weddings in the past year or who planned to be married before the issue went to press. My job was to coordinate the photos and interviews before the deadline, in ten weeks—a massive organizational feat. When I sat at my desk the day after the first phone conference, I realized that I could not look at the long-term goal: the finished magazine with all the stories and photos. When I thought of the immensity of the effort required to get there, I became despondent. I'd need to make a minimum of ten phone calls for each of these couples, check and double-check all the way down to the wire. It was like being in sales. What I had to do, instead of staring at the floor in defeat at the approaching deadline, was to get on the phone.

I got a new call book from the magazine's stationery supply closet and labeled it "Weddings." In it I wrote down all the publicists, wedding planners, journalists, agents, dress designers, florists, hairstylists, makeup artists, photographers, and caterers I had to call, with their phone numbers next to their names. I did just as the business goal setters recommend. Every time I reached someone, I put a check next to the name. If the issue between us was resolved, I put two checks next to the name. At the end of the day, I moved all the single-checked and unchecked names to a new page. Sixty lines per page meant sixty names. In the beginning my daily list stretched past two pages.

As we got nearer to the publication day, I could see evidence that focusing on the thing that was close at hand and had to be done immediately was a much more productive way of achieving a goal. Gradually my list of carryover phone calls shrunk to half a page, and I could feel relief. The goal that was unimaginable nine weeks before was close to accomplished. This did not completely prevent last-minute anxiety, of course. As the publication date neared, there were rumors that five of the forty couples, some of whom had been married only a few months, might divorce before we got the magazine to the printers. Despite all this planning, meeting daily and weekly goals, I was still dealing with a situation I could not completely control.

Although most writers will never work on their books the way I did on *People*'s weddings issue, the point is that before a piece of writing is finished, there are hundreds of smaller tasks and bigger ones that have to be completed, and it doesn't do you much good to keep your eye on a goal that's way off on the horizon. The goal may in its grandest terms be to write the great American novel. Still, you have to do the little stuff first. You must break down the monolith into individual milestones.

My newspaper friends and I used to laugh at the many stories we had to write about the notion of setting achievable goals. Most times, the experts we featured in these stories promoted the idea of setting goals that were so commonplace as to be ridiculous. "My goal today," one of my wiseguy friends once announced, "is to put on my pants." Then he looked down at his legs and proclaimed, "Done!" (Now that I work from home, I see that putting on your pants is not an insignificant goal!) Smaller goals are not to be derided along the pathway to finishing your writing. The immediate tasks and problems to be solved may be humble, but only through completing the small tasks consistently can you approach the goal that is on the distant horizon.

In finishing his novel, Cary realized his first job was to bring some order to the process, but he had devised a new method with Finishing School. Each Saturday, instead of dreaming about having a book on the shelf in his favorite bookstore, he looked at the time he had in the week ahead and the list of tasks he needed to complete to finish his novel by the end of the year. Setting a weekly goal is not all grim business. It allows for pure creative work. The task he chose in one recent week was to figure out a way to get his characters from point A to point B.

The goal is small and defined but can still cause a frizz of fear when you sit down to write. This frightening and difficult creative power delights in contrariness and surprise, and not doing the obvious. You are at its mercy. All you can do in the case of a goal like Cary's is say that you are going to get these people from point A to point B and that you want to do it in an interesting and artful way and find some joy in it. He put that on the top of his page to use as a prompt when he started to write.

For Cary's week with this plot problem, he might list all the different motivations a character could have for making this journey. One character's motivation could be his childhood. Perhaps he was being blackmailed. Maybe this trip was a secret dream he'd had his whole life. Or there was something the readers don't know about him that's also hidden from the other characters. Someone else is making him do it. His father always did this so he thinks he should. He needs the money. His wife is nagging him to do it. Exploring the character's possible motivations by making a list was a systematic, rigorous stretching of the imagination. Cary could review the list the next time he sat down and realize that while most of the possible motivations were false, or even silly, one choice felt exactly right. He had been logical in listing the choices, but the final decision he turned over to intuition.

This is a small decision, but it is an important one and one that shows steady progress toward the goal in the way that Oettingen says is the surest route to success. You start with a dream, but to make the dream a reality you take it apart into its smaller pieces, bits that you can accomplish week by week, that you choose carefully with the support of your creative buddies in Finishing School. The small-scale goal gives you the delight of incremental victories, a confidence in steady progress in measurable ways.

The Finishing School sessions permit you to get lost too, to really sit in the mystery of creativity. For those who have not worked on their writing for a long time, the first goal may be, as in picking up the rock of the paragraph, just to sit with the physical product of your creativity, to handle it and catalog it, consider it and trust that you will develop a strategy for beginning to write again. If you say, "I'm going to write my novel by the end of summer," that is a noble goal, but without a plan it will remain just that.

Dreaming is beautiful but dreaming is not enough. Being

reasonable about goals is being reasonable about who you are and what you bring to the creative endeavor. Making a logical assessment of your creative ability reveals the obstacles in your way, external and internal. Meeting your week-by-week goals, you may get to the end of the year without finishing your novel, but you will be pleased with yourself because of the solid progress you made by working steadily throughout the year.

Writing Day by Day

Danelle

I NEVER PROCLAIM my method of managing time as a program or a solution for others, because I see what works for me as idiosyncratic. I started my writing life as a journalist, and it is easy for me to toggle between one project and another, even between three or four at the same time. I know this is difficult for people who like to get lost in their work and lose track of time. That is mostly unappealing to me, and my time-management system reflects that taste. Telling someone else they will succeed in managing their time better if they do as I do is like saying the way for you to get more things done is to be me. I wouldn't advocate that to anyone. Yet talking to Cary about this made me realize that for many people time management is an enormous struggle and another source of writing shame. I don't think about it very much because my system works for me.

I've known Cary for many years and rarely have I seen him lean in with such interest as he did when I described how I manage my time. For those who struggle with time management, the whole process is a mystery. When I described what I see as simple techniques, it was as if I had stood up in Cary's living room and moved aside a bookcase to reveal a hidden passage to a secret world. "Really?" he said with absolute bafflement. "You make a list and you stick to it? Amazing." He asked me to write down how I do it, so here goes.

EVERY MORNING, AFTER I meditate, I make a list of things I want to accomplish that day. First I write down everything that comes to mind, including some things I may have done already. I like to check things off right away, to enjoy the feeling of getting the momentum going. Here's an annotated list:

1. Laundry

I'd already done most of the laundry. I just had to get it from the dryer downstairs, in the collective space, something I'd not done the night before. I wrote this here so I'd be able to check it off when I completed the task before I sat down to write.

2. Call Roland

Call stepfather, must be done early in the morning when he's at his best. Easy to check off too.

3. Humor column

This was the most important thing I had to do that day and the most fun!

4. Joy M.

Review new chapter from a woman I'm collaborating with and send her notes.

5. Trains calls

Calls to railroad companies for feature piece I'm writing.

6. Gym

7. Harvey

Chat with prospective client, who also required a lengthy e-mail specifying what you get if you hire me to write your book proposal.

8. Talk with BD, 1:00 p.m.

Conference call with prospective client and acquiring editor of the new book.

9. Reread FSB chapters and send to Cary

Final review of small pieces of writing for the Finishing School *book before sending them to Cary.*

10. Blog post p.m.

Had drafted the blog post but needed to review it before it could go live.

Next I look at the tasks and estimate how much time they each will take and what kind of mood I might be in after completing them. Calling the same five railroad people, who never are there and don't return my phone calls, takes five minutes.

Reviewing Joy's chapter I estimated at an hour and a half, and an hour to reread the stuff for Cary. I wasn't sure how long the phone calls with Harvey and BD would take, but I thought no more than half an hour each. I decided to do all the short tasks of reviewing and phone calling in the morning so the afternoon, after the call with BD, would be free for a more quiet and expansive kind of work: the fun and creativity of working on the humor column.

I knocked out the first tasks pretty quickly. Joy M.'s review and rereading the pieces for Cary took less time than I'd budgeted. The call to Harvey took longer than I expected, as did writing the e-mail to him, giving me not enough time to go to the gym before the BD call at one. The gym is the part of the schedule that regularly goes undone, and my big butt tells that tale. After BD, I took a walk and came back to spend the rest of the day on the humor column. At that point it was too late to work on the blog post, so I rolled that item over and had the first task for the next day's list.

I HAVE A few other general rules.

If I have something unpleasant to do, such as calling someone with whom I'm going to have a difficult conversation, I do it first. I know from long experience that delaying that call doesn't make it any easier. I don't like the dull foreboding that dominates the day when you keep delaying the unpleasant encounter. For me, something like that would definitely affect my ability to be playful with a piece of writing like the humor column. When Cary and I were talking about how I manage my time, he found this aspect of time management to be worth noting; that when I'm looking at the things I'd like to get accomplished on a given day, I slot them in the pleasant or unpleasant column so I acknowledge the difference between the things I'm eager to do and those I dread. He said, to my surprise, most people don't look at their days that way. They do the thing they want to do and get wrapped up in it until something else demands their attention. I find that remarkable, probably as remarkable as my method might seem to people with time-management issues.

Now, LOOKING AT how I manage my time, I see several specific actions, taken from my intuitive response to this challenge, that can be described as a method:

1. Make a list. List everything, including the small stuff like phoning a relative or taking out the recycling. Experience the quick satisfaction of checking off some tasks right away. Plus you always have an answer to the question, where did the day go? You know exactly how much you got done. Little tasks can end up taking a lot more time than you expect.

2. Assign value to the tasks. Will this task be fun or a drag? If it's fun and you want to spend more time on it, allot more time to it and structure the day in a way to protect that time. If it's a drag, get it over with right away so the whole day is not colored by it. This way you can alternate unpleasant or less intriguing work with stuff you like. That way the day has,

over all, variation and rhythm. You can look forward to the afternoon, when you've cleared your desk and have time for play and creativity.

3. Estimate how much time each task will take, and try to hold yourself to that timeline. This is not always possible but, with practice, you will find it is more doable than not. The more you focus on the actual amount of time a task takes, the easier it is to take control of your day.

4. Never despair about the things you didn't get to. Life rarely cooperates with your plans. Someone unexpected calls you and sends you into a reverie, or you get upsetting news from a family member that takes up a big chunk of the day. There is always tomorrow, which you acknowledge when you shift the tasks you didn't complete to the next day's list and figure out how you can fit them in.

Something that disrupts this daily plan is our old friend the unconscious, but for me this usually is a positive interruption. Once or twice a month I wake up with my mind already engaged in one of my ongoing projects. As my conscious mind surfaces from sleep, it's already creating jokes or has an insight that's going to clarify a tricky passage in one of my collaborations. I always go with that, a thing I call "morning mind." Morning mind is that clear, pure energy of a brain that has not yet been polluted by the many interactions of the day—the e-mails on your phone and the visits to Facebook. If that mind is running free, I run with it for as long as it lasts (usually no more than two hours) and then get down to making my list.

The attitude at the bottom of this is what I think will be hard to replicate for those who have time-management problems. That attitude—confining my time commitments to a defined number of hours or minutes—can be very hard for others to adopt. In my experience, my ability to work effectively on a particular project has limits. The most I can give a piece of writing is three or four hours. Typically, my juice starts to run low at about two hours. If I stay longer on it, I get trapped in repetitive thoughts, sometimes drop into self-abuse, and then begin to think of the work I did as mediocre.

HERE'S A GOOD example of this, which illustrates the difference between Cary and me in our writing and time-management approaches.

We agreed to complete the same assignment: to write a paragraph about each of the emotional pitfalls: doubt, shame, yearning, fear, judgment, and arrogance. We each approached it in a very different way.

I decided I would sit down and let 'er rip. We've all got plenty of experience of shame around writing and all the other emotions. The best way to do this assignment was automatic writing, I thought. Narrate my own yearning or arrogance without trying to pretty it up, make me sound appealing, or make a coherent argument or deep insight. The appeal of it for me was the freedom to be my worst self and air those miserable monologues for the benefit of all. I gave myself an hour, ten minutes for each emotion, and actually finished before the hour was up because it was so liberating to be that naked.

When we met the next week, Cary hadn't worked on this

part of our assignments. He had written it down on his list and done all the others, but something kept him away from this one. When we talked about it, it was clear that what kept him from the emotion assignment was that he didn't want to get too wrapped up in it. He feared that if he started on it, emotion would envelop him, and he'd be overcome with those feelings, which would make him completely unproductive for the rest of the day. The day would elapse with nothing done except him experiencing the debilitating insecurity of shame or doubt, etc.—something he works pretty hard to keep at bay.

I think many will say that Cary is right. You open the door to that kind of thing and you can forget about the rest of the day, maybe even the week. And many would identify with the kind of writer he is, someone who gets lost in the depth of feeling and finds that hours pass with him just staring blankly as emotions overtake his body. Some might say that's a better, truer, and more classical way to create—to do so in an open-ended way and give it plenty of time so you can see what emerges.

I've worked with hundreds of writers in my career as a collaborator, and I never think that anyone's process is superior. People work the way they work, and a process that would drive me absolutely mad—like my friend who cuts up her chapter draft into sentences and moves the sentences around after laying them out on top of her bed—is as essential to them as my list is to me. I never criticize another writer's method, just as I do not advocate that someone try to adopt mine. For me, the way Cary starts writing, with a mind and schedule that will remain open for as long as it requires, would drive me batty, and I bet my method would feel so confining as to inhibit his creativity.

Know thyself is the key here. Even if I were to allot the whole morning to writing about one of those emotions, it would still likely take just the ten minutes I reserved for it in my original plan. I work better if there are limits on my time. Confining this task to one hour meant that I looked forward to it as an opportunity for self-expression in a day filled with working on other people's writing. And there is always the possibility that I will get so caught up in what I'm writing that I'll neglect the other items and just go with the inspiration. Being the way I am, that happens only about once a month. It means when it does happen, I am grateful that, on balance, I get so much done. Those other people on my schedule can wait a day. I'm a writer, and sometimes you just have to go where the writing takes you. Having a schedule and mostly sticking to it doesn't prevent that from happening.

Part 4

How to Create
Your Own Finishing
School

The Crisis That Created
Finishing School

Cary

In 2006 I was in a dark period in my life as a writer. On the outside I looked good. But I was not happy. Writing did not feel right.

I was gaining fame as *Salon*'s advice columnist. I had taken over the job from writer and radio host Garrison Keillor in 2001 and was writing the "Since You Asked" column five days a week, working from home with very little editorial interference. It was a dream job, and I was lucky to have it. But I was not happy and relaxed *while doing the work*.

Plus, I had recently suffered a panic attack while writing and had ended up in the hospital.

The panic attack persuaded me to seek insight into why I was in such turmoil about my writing. Up until I was lying in a hospital bed, being checked for evidence of a heart attack, I had assumed my problem of writerly anxiety was unique, which means I hadn't really thought about it at all. I knew that writers famously tended to drink a lot and have social-adjustment problems, but I had never followed this thinking to its inevitable and logical conclusion: if writers famously had these problems, then someone, somewhere, some writer, must have written literary essays about the very kinds of stresses I was enduring. This was one of those Homer Simpson "d'oh!" moments. Might not other writers of skill and repute have also suffered this anxiety—this brittle, nervous, impatient alternation between arrogance and low self-esteem—and written about it in ways that might give me some insight and possible relief?

Of course! And where would I find such writing? Possibly in a bookstore?

This was the kind of reasonable, problem-solving thought that a normal, well-balanced person might have. Needless to say, I was not that person. For me, it took having a panic attack and ending up in the hospital.

Furthermore, a normal, well-adjusted person would then simply go into a bookstore and see what books are available about this topic. For me, going into a bookstore was another problem. This requires more embarrassing truth telling: I was so overly concerned about my status as a totally cool person (read: massive unacknowledged insecurity!) that I would actually *not buy certain books or records if I feared my purchase might make me look uncool in the eyes of the store clerk.*

As I say, on the outside I looked good. I was an internationally known columnist praised for the quality of his thought on a host of personal, psychological, and emotional issues. But I was also so immature that before making a bookstore purchase

I would actually rehearse the explanation I might need if my purchase was not deemed sufficiently cool. So what happened? One day my neurotic anxiety and self-hatred just got to be too much. It broke like a fever.

I screwed up my courage and went to Borders to browse in the writing section.

This was heresy. A real writer did not read books on how to be a writer. A real writer didn't need advice. I was the one giving the advice! Yet I steeled myself for the walk through Borders to the section on writing. I remember cringing, scrunching my shoulders, keeping my head down lest I be recognized. I went down the aisle, and one title caught my eye. It was called *Writing Alone and with Others*. What an odd and interesting title, I thought—a literary-sounding title, quiet and grammatical and sensible yet also odd and surprising.

I took it off the shelf and looked inside. Though I had never heard of the author, I read some of her words in the book and I liked her voice. Pat Schneider was the founder of the Amherst Writers and Artists workshop. Her prose was direct, quiet, clear, forceful, level, passionate. It felt true and unpretentious. What I found was more than advice; she offered an actual method to bring writers together to write. Writing together! How strange and interesting an idea. How utterly counterintuitive. I felt in my chest a sense of hope and promise. I did not know ahead of time that this was what I was looking for, yet it drew me to it, and I purchased the book.

I read the book on a plane trip to Germany. A few months later I was in Berkeley, taking Pat Schneider's weeklong workshop in the AWA method.

———

By the fall of 2007 I was leading my first AWA workshop in the living room of our San Francisco house.

For the next eight years, I led those workshops and doing that changed how I felt about writing and about other writers and readers. By focusing on each writer's unique voice, and encouraging respect and support for writing as a craft, the AWA workshops gave me a new, vibrant, healthy way to relate to my own creative self. It's fair to say that the AWA method saved my creative life.

But there was one more piece to the puzzle. That's where Finishing School was born.

The AWA method helps participants overcome their fears and insecurities about writing, so they can write freely and joyfully in their own way. It had worked wonders for me and others, but I was left frustrated in one respect: as a group, we were not sending our work out for publication, nor were we working steadily, month after month, toward the goal of completing major works.

I myself was stalled on a long novel project. I also had a habit of beginning smaller works but not taking them to completion and submitting them for publication. As I related earlier in talking about my family history, this habit held great personal shame for me.

I decided to see if I could use the same group process but toward a different goal: that of completing and submitting work. I wanted to use the AWA principles of support and respect to help people achieve a more externally defined, tangible result. Workshop participants would crystallize their vision, schedule time to work toward it with mutual support, and work steadily to get their writing finished, polished, and published.

The final piece of the puzzle was finding a way to add accountability without judgment.

Twenty years earlier, my friend Alan Kaufman and I had attended some meetings in San Francisco of the group Artists Recovering through the Twelve Steps (ARTS) Anonymous. Alan and I became "art buddies." As such, we would meet every Wednesday afternoon and send out our work together. We would go to the post office together.

This was an amazing revelation for me and also, I think, for Alan. We recognized how difficult even this simple act of sending out our work was and how concrete and material it was. The matters of copies and stamps and envelopes were of prime importance. That was really all it was: stamps, envelopes, copies, and standing in line at the post office. It was the doing of it. It was completely material. It wasn't magic. This knowledge, gained through experience, rooted us. It made us workers in the field of literature and gave us great confidence and also made us confront our enormous fears and desires for escape. We boosted each other and cheered each other on. It was weirdly terrifying and yet exhilarating to go to the post office with our shabby, strange poems, to seek out publications that might take our work. It was Alan, actually, who encouraged me to submit my story "When Life Was Wild" to the Canadian literary magazine *McGill Street,* and that was the story that grew into my novel *Famous Actress Disappears.* So this novel, which I finished using the Finishing School method, actually grew out of the same experiences that Finishing School itself grew out of.

The lessons Alan and I learned by attending meetings of ARTS Anonymous stuck with me. Making your intentions known, committing to them, having an art buddy: these were genuinely useful things. Drawing on these lessons, I knew we could find a way that we could mutually encourage each other and provide a structure that would get us to completing our work and sending it out.

Finishing School for Two

Cary

WHAT IF YOU want to use the Finishing School method on your own? You can do Finishing School for two. All you need is a Finishing School buddy.

Your buddy doesn't have to be a friend. Your buddy doesn't have to be an expert. All that is required is that your buddy be willing to follow the method.

Pick someone you think would be a good creative buddy and explain the Finishing School method. Ask them to join you. Or spread the word among coworkers and family members. Place an ad in Craigslist. Place notices on bulletin boards in cafés and other places where creative people congregate. The notice might say something like this:

"Are you interested in finishing a writing project that you have put off? If so, please contact me to see about working together to each finish a project, using the Finishing School method. It's free! It's fun!"

When someone expresses interest or wants to know more, we suggest sending a note like the following:

Dear [name of friend, interested person, etc.],

Thank you for expressing interest in working with me to finish something.

What I am suggesting is that you join with me in a monthlong program of mutual support in which each of us will help the other get something done. We meet once a week for four weeks. It's totally free. It's based on the book *Finishing School* by Cary Tennis and Danelle Morton.

Please let me know if you are willing and interested, and I will send you more information and suggest some times when we can meet.

Signed,

Your Potential Finishing School Buddy

If your prospect responds positively, then make plans to meet. Ask that before you meet, your prospect write down answers to the following questions:

- What is the name of your project? (Giving it a name really seems to help.)
- What type of project are you working on? (Genre, medium, subject area.)
- How long have you been working on it?
- How long will you need to completely finish it?
- What part of it would you like to finish this month?
- If this part has components, what are the components?

If you don't get this information ahead of time, you can go over it at the first meeting instead.

Then agree on a time and place where you can meet once a week for four weeks. Allow one hour for each meeting. At the first meeting, give your partner this written pledge. Ask them to read it over and, if they are willing, to sign it:

Dear Friend,

To indicate that each of us is serious and committed to finishing, we make this agreement.

We agree, to the best of our ability

- that each of us has something he or she very much desires to finish;
- that we will sincerely try this method;
- and that we will work toward finishing something important to us.

Therefore I agree

- to meet with my creative buddy in person for one hour, once a week, for four weeks at an agreed-upon place and time;
- to record in a calendar, either paper or digital, our meeting times and also the times I am committing to work on my project;
- to e-mail, phone, or text my partner at the beginning and end of each of my work sessions;
- and that because this is not a critique group, I will not ask my partner to read and/or critique my work, and I will not offer to critique my partner's work.

After you have met and are settled, ask your buddy if they are ready, and then say, "Okay, we're now having a Finishing School meeting." Ask your partner to describe their project and what they hope to finish this month.

Listen until you understand exactly what the goal is, and then restate it so you are sure you have heard correctly.

Often a person's first goals will be overly ambitious, but let them discover that on their own. The beauty of Finishing School is that just by following the method, we learn about our habits, strengths, and shortcomings.

After your partner has described their project, ask them what time they have available for it. Ask your partner to slot times on their calendar for the week and show them to you. Ask your partner to e-mail, text, or call you before and after each work session.

Then report to your partner in a similar manner. Describe your project, define what you hope to accomplish in the month, say what parts of it you are going to work on this week, and show your partner where you have written in the times you plan to work. Make sure you have your partner's correct contact info. Tell them they can expect to hear from you.

If there is time after you have settled all that, spend it talking about your past experiences with unfinished tasks or things you have learned about the subject. When this is the topic, the discussions can go beyond the boundary of the single hour you have agreed to spend each week in Finishing School. If you see that you've passed the one-hour mark, ask permission to continue. Unless you both agree to extend the time together, separate and agree to meet again next week. If the sessions go outside the boundaries too often, you and/or your partner may be resentful of that. It's best to be clear on the rules and on when you are bending them. That's a good habit in the partnership you've just established as well as in your writing.

That is for the first week.

If it is the second or third week, ask how the week went. Ask if they completed their stated goals.

Listen as your partner discusses how it went, whether well or poorly. Invite your partner to talk about the experience, but refrain from offering suggestions or advice. If things went well, congratulate them. If your partner did not meet their goals for the week, ask what went wrong and what changes they are contemplating, if any, but do not offer helpful hints or scolding, even in jest. Just be level, interested, and reassuring.

In every regular Finishing School session there is a leader. The leader shares goals with others, reports on progress, and checks in with a creative buddy just like everybody else.

In Finishing School for two, it is a little different. In a group, when the leader shares, no one individual feels a responsibility to respond because it's a group. It's not that personal. But with just two people, as you sit across from this person and listen to them share their experience, there is a natural felt responsibility to respond, to, in effect, take on the role of leader. So just try to mirror what the leader has done, asking what the project is, how the week went, remaining neutral, refraining from offering advice, etc.

————

THESE SUGGESTIONS APPLY to both people in Finishing School
for two:

- Stick to asking how it went: Did you meet your goal?
  What obstacles did you encounter? How are you feeling
  about it? What are your plans for the upcoming week?
- Try not to volunteer advice. If asked for your opinion,
  ask yourself if you have had a similar experience and recount what happened.
- Be a good interviewer: Listen. Say as little as possible. Let
  your partner puzzle out their own experience.
- Be positive and encouraging about the results you hear.
- In relating your experience, stick to the facts: what you
  did, what happened.
- Resist the temptation to ask to see the work or share your
  own. This is not a critique session. If your partner needs
  a critique group, an editor, or some kind of consulting
  help, suggest that they make finding that person or group
  a task to work on in Finishing School.
- It is fine to commiserate, to say, "Gee, that's tough," or "I
  understand how that can be," but resist the impulse to jump
  in and relate a similar experience of your own right away.
- Keep in mind that this might be the first time your
  partner has talked about this area of life. It might be unexpectedly emotional. Do not pry. You're not a therapist.
  Do not analyze your partner. Your job is only to be a supportive witness.

When sharing, try to just say what happened and mention what you plan to do next time, without going into your whole history of fear and procrastination. When mentioning obstacles, try to say something like "Because of the fear that cropped up last week, this week I'm going to try to acknowledge the fear if it comes up but just keep working."

If the two of you feel like you are finished before the time is up, we suggest you stay there and do whatever work you can. If there is some writing or list making to do, do it there, together, so you are using the full hour to make progress on your project. You may be surprised at how much tangible progress you can make. Staying for the full hour also reinforces for you, subconsciously, or emotionally, the fact that *you have that full hour available to you to do this work that is vitally important to you. You have made it available. It shows that you can schedule time and use it.* If you quit early, it undermines the solemnity of the event; it gives the subtle signal that this meeting is just another somewhat casual event. Formality of structure and regularity are what the subconscious craves, so give yourself that. Use the time you have scheduled.

When your hour is up, confirm, before leaving, the time and place that you will meet again next week. Make sure you and your partner have both written into your calendars the times you are going to work.

It is a tradition in my in-house workshops to make a little celebration of the last meeting. It is satisfying to print out what we have accomplished and declare it done, dropping it to the wood floor so it makes a resounding SMACK! If you are doing Finishing School for two, on the last day make it special. Print out your work and bring it along to show. Drop it to the floor, if appropriate, to hear that satisfying sound. Celebrate with a dinner or an exchange of gifts, or some soul-satisfying experience such as a concert or movie. Make it special.

How to Set Up a Full-Scale
Finishing School
of Your Own

Danelle

CARY AND I believed the idea behind Finishing School was so simple that it would be easy for others to set up their own classes wherever they lived. Certainly Cary had proved, when he devised the method, that all he had to do was announce it and people started to volunteer to take his class. Cary had been teaching writing for many years and had a pool of appreciative students whom he could ask if they wanted to try it out, but the question remained of how you would do it if you were not Cary.

What if you had no student base, or even any connection to the world of writing classes, and you'd never taught anything before? Was it plausible that someone like that—meaning me, Danelle—could be successful in establishing her own Finishing School?

Cary moved to Italy while we were writing this book, leaving the field open for me to attempt this experiment, and

I confess the whole idea made me very nervous. Mainly I was nervous about marketing, or, rather, I was nervous that I would do all kinds of inventive things to get the idea before strangers and still no one would sign up to take my class. What follows is my experience setting up Finishing School for those of you who feel inspired by the book to try it.

First I had to figure out what kind of a commitment I wanted to make and where I would conduct the class. As I was teaching it for the first time, I decided that to encourage people to come I would offer the first two weeks of class for free. This meant no risk for the students and little risk for me. I considered the possibilities that I would not be a very good teacher or that I would not enjoy it. If I tried it out for two classes and either no one came or I realized I was not looking forward to the meeting, I could cancel it without having bruised too many feelings.

Like Cary, I decided to hold the class in my home. I live in an economically depressed town that does not have cafés that are open late enough to be suited for this kind of gathering, and I also thought the café setting might inhibit people from feeling completely free to talk about the problems they were having with their writing. Home seemed the best. I had a friend make a flyer that had a Gmail address and my telephone number. I strolled around the modest town where I live and asked the owners of cafés and galleries if they would post the flyer in their windows.

I enjoyed walking around downtown handing out the flyer. I got a chance to speak with the owners of the cafés and restaurants, people I see but rarely have a chance to talk with. Many of them knew someone who had a friend they thought might be interested in the class, and in one case an employee had a partially completed short story that he was interested in working on. This really boosted my mood about the appeal of the class.

I announced the class on Facebook as well as on other community forums I visit, like Nextdoor. I searched Facebook for pages that focus on community activities and writing groups in my area and investigated how to announce the class on those pages. Sometimes you need permission from an administrator, and that takes a few days to secure. By far the most successful marketing came from posting something on Meetup. The Meetup site allows you to announce an event and choose tags for it that will send messages to people who are interested in the topic of the meeting. The tags I chose were <u>Science Fiction Writing</u> · <u>Writer's Block</u> · <u>Fiction</u> · <u>Creative Writing</u> · <u>Authors</u> · <u>Artists</u> · <u>Writing</u> · <u>Writing Workshops</u> · <u>Playwriting, Screenwriting</u> · <u>Novel Writing</u> · <u>Short Story Writing</u> · <u>Fiction Writing</u> · <u>Memoir Writing; Life Writing</u> · <u>Book Writing</u>. I posted the notice on January 2 and described the idea and me:

> *Do you have a creative project that has a claim on your heart but somehow you just can't seem to finish it? You may be stalled at the beginning, trapped in the middle, or frightened of the end. Wherever you are in the process, the answer is Finishing School. I am the coauthor of fifteen books, three of them best sellers. With my writing partner, Cary Tennis, I've sold a book about Finishing School to Penguin Books for publication this fall. I'm offering small weekly workshops in my Vallejo home featuring this exciting new way to break through your blocks to get your work started again and finished.*

Here's how I described the first class:

Come to the first meeting with your calendar open, spirits high, and join with other creative people in an encouraging spirit of collaboration. We will define times in our week when we can commit to working and decide realistically how much we can do in those hours. We'll choose creative buddies who can support us in meeting those goals despite the many responsibilities and surprises that conspire to stop us. And when we meet again the next week, we'll share our success in fulfilling those goals and set new ones. As we're just getting started in Vallejo, the first two weeks are free, so give this a try. It can be the first step to realizing your creative ambitions.

A week later twenty people had expressed interest in Finishing School, and seven signed up to attend the first class.

This made me extremely happy in that it was a great market test for interest in the idea, but it set off a bit of panic in me. I had not thought anyone would be interested, and the fact that so quickly twenty were made me fear I would not be able to accommodate all the interested people in my small loft. I thought about it for a while before deciding that I had to limit the number of people to ten, and not just because that's an amount that can fit comfortably in the apartment. The format of the class is that we determine how much time we have in the week ahead, describe where we are in our projects, and then choose a reasonable goal for the week. This means that everyone in the class gets individual attention tailored to their project. If there were more than ten people, it would be impossible to really attend to each one, and I would be very conscious of the time, rather than being able to stay with the person until we came up with a solution for him or her.

I got a little compulsive about checking the Meetup page to see who had RSVP'd and who had recently joined. Some of the people who joined had photos posted next to their names, and I was intrigued by thinking that all these people would be in my living room. People I'd never met would be leaving their houses on a Thursday night and driving some distance to join up with other people who wanted to finish. I got excited thinking about it and a little nervous about whether I'd be able to be as effective a teacher as Cary had been for my class.

I chose to start on the third Thursday of the month, to allow plenty of time to get enough students for the class. Midway through the month the class was full, with a waiting list, and thirty-two people were signed up on the Meetup page.

I'd also gone to a meeting of local artists who were concerned about an upcoming city council action and passed out my flyer there. Some people at that meeting expressed interest, inspiring visions of dozens of people crammed into my apartment, restive in the hallway, a line down the stairs, perhaps a velvet rope.

In truth, seven students showed up to my first class, which was plenty.

IN THE HOURS before the class, I fussed around, cleaning and ensuring that there were tea and coffee and something to snack on, as I would provide for any guest. All the while I was bustling around, I was jotting down notes for what I would say to introduce the class to these students. Here's my list:

- *Thank you*
- *Happy*
- *Grateful*
- *Acknowledge nobility of what we are trying to do*
- *We come as equals, each of us learns from each other*
- *Finishing School book due in April and this class will be part of it*
- *History of how Finishing School came about*
- *Method and rationale*
- *Take away the bullshit from writing and take the work, not ourselves, seriously*
- *Take census of group and projects. Where are they in the process?*
- *Ask them to get out calendars and begin.*

I recorded my opening remarks, most of which I'm pasting in here so you can take any cues that are helpful to you if you want to address your class. I'm an extrovert and enjoy speaking, so likely I went on a bit longer than an introvert would.

Hi and welcome. It's a noble thing that you are trying to do, to write. You may doubt yourself and think that you are arrogant to assume you have something to say that is worth listening to, but I think the reverse is the truth. You are humble in the goal to fulfill that dream. You've worked hard, and you're willing to work harder because there is something you need to say. It's not about the other people who may or may not be paying attention. It's about you and the desire to touch someone else's humanity with your experience, and that is a noble goal that you should never lose.

We come as equals to Finishing School. The struggle you have completing your work is the same as the one that published writers like me do. We all face the same issues of arrogance, fear, judgment, shame, yearning, and doubt. The way we address these problems in our work is something we can learn from. We all can learn from each other, and the spirit of the class is egalitarian.

Finishing School is Cary Tennis's creation, and I was one of his first students. He saw that many people in his writing classes were having creative breakthroughs but only a few of them were finishing their work, and he could count himself among them. This is why he developed the very simple method of Finishing School.

Let me explain the method. We meet once a week and consult our calendars to identify the hours when we can write. The point is to make a commitment you can keep. Do not be overly ambitious and decide to impress yourself or the class by committing to more hours than you can reasonably work. If it's only an hour you can write, take that hour and use it and be proud of it. This means you did it. You kept your word and you wrote.

After we know how many hours you have to work, you pick a task in your writing that is appropriate for that amount of time. If you define what you are going to do when you sit down to write, it greatly increases the odds that you're going to come away from that session feeling better about yourself. Finishing School helps you make your focus clear.

The third piece of this is the creative buddy. We'll exchange cell numbers before class is over, and I'll match you with someone else in the class. When you sit down to write, you text your buddy to let them know, and that person will text you too when they start to write. This seems minor but it's a big part of what makes the program work. It's a simple form of accountability that reminds you that someone wants you to succeed. When you do not feel like writing, you can think of the people who expect that you will. It's one of the things that can get you back to work.

When we come together next week, we will not read each other's writing. We will only discuss whether we wrote, what got in the way of that, and recommit to what we want to accomplish in the next week. That's it. I know it sounds a bit too simple, but the simplest solutions are often the most effective. I took Finishing School from Cary in 2013 and finished the first draft of a book proposal I'd been struggling with for more than a year. If you truly follow this method, you will finish because it gives you a way to cut the bullshit away from the work and take it, and not yourself, seriously. So let's everybody get out their calendars.

Then I took a survey to see in general what people were working on. Six people were working on fiction and one was working on a nonfiction piece. Five were writing a book and two had shorter pieces in mind. Two people were just starting, while the others had between ten thousand and forty thousand words written. I asked how long each one had been working on his or her piece, and everyone said years.

EIGHT OF US met, and each one had a different problem in his or her writing. One was just starting out and had paragraphs scattered all over the place and didn't know where to start, whether to start writing or to review these bits and pieces. Another had three chapters and a plan for a whole book, but every time she sat down to write she compared herself to the writers she admired and would end up spending her writing time telling herself that she'd never be a writer. Another person had completed a novel that didn't get much response. His writer self was wounded and he didn't know if he had the courage to write again, but he missed it. He missed looking up and seeing that the sun was rising and realizing he'd been writing all night. It was amazing how candid everyone was and how different all their writing lives were.

We picked partners by tossing slips of paper with our names and cell phone numbers on them into a hat. Assignment is completely random. If the numbers are uneven, or someone drops out of the class, we discuss aloud how to include the stray partner in another circle. Usually people are in pairs, but as there is an odd number in my class right now, we are a trio and we are all on a group text message. I'm an equal to them, and we all announce to the other two when any of us is writing.

Most of the students entered my apartment with fearful looks on their faces, and when they spoke about their writing they were ashamed. When they left, everyone was smiling, eager to get to work. I heard a few of them standing around on the street, below my window, laughing. I could not be happier to have helped them restore joy to their work, and every one of them committed to the next meeting. It was a great night!

At the second class meeting, two of the first students did not come and were replaced by two more first-time students, so we still had seven. The meeting proceeded similarly to the first one, without the lengthy speech, and everyone exchanged numbers and agreed to tasks. I also wanted to crowdsource how much people were willing to pay, which you might want to do too if you are thinking of conducting your own Finishing School. Cary had charged $170 a month in San Francisco, and I would have paid more, considering the results I achieved. Here in Vallejo, I knew that was way too much for the people who would be attending my classes. I passed around blank pieces of paper and asked the students to write down how much they were willing to pay each month for the class. The answers ranged from $40 to $100 with more in the bottom range than the top.

I was a bit disappointed by this, because I wanted to charge $100. Instead of averaging the price around $50, I chose to charge $75, and at the next class I had only two students. As I write this, I'm on the fence about whether this was the right decision. When I think it was the right one, I assure myself that those who are willing to pay $75 will find their way to me and that those people will really value the class because they are willing to spend that money. It's got to hurt a little or they are not serious. At the moments when I regret it and wish I had decided to charge less, I think of the single mom with a teenage son she had to dump off at the Boys and Girls Club so she could make the class. Everything in her life hurts a little, and she was making a big effort even if she couldn't pay much money to come. That Saturday I texted her and offered to give her a single-mom discount but she did not return to class.

In my three months teaching Finishing School, I've come to see that it is not a class for everyone who wants to write, only those who are serious about their work and willing to face what they learn about themselves in the process of completing it. This turns out to be a small but dedicated number of people.

Finishing School cannot take away the pain of remembering. If your memories make you tremble and want to run, and if doing your work involves facing such memories, you may find yourself turning away from them in a number of ways and quitting Finishing School because it is too hard.

A woman started my class very enthusiastically because she saw how the plain format of Finishing School might get her out of the place where she was stuck writing about a painful incident. In the second week of class, she shared that working on her memoir had been difficult, as it had called up memories about people from whom she was estranged and cruel things that family members had done to her. In class she expressed gratitude that she had the support of her creative buddy and advice from me and the other members of the class in beginning this work. There was something shaky about the way she recounted this progress, as if it had not been as enjoyable as she was portraying it to be. She did not return to class in the third week and e-mailed me to say that she had found a different writers' group closer to her home. I sensed, in the abruptness of her exit and the unlikeliness of her explanation, that some force within her had taken her away. When Cary heard this, he said, "That's the bear!"

The students who remain in class are dedicated to their craft and to the goal of writing every week. In mood, spirit, and word count they are making strong and steady progress. The class has given them a place where people take their dream seriously and never question how they are going to accomplish it. Not everyone is ready for that. Not everyone truly wants to finish. Finishing School works best when everyone is ready to make the commitment to finishing.

Tips for a Leader: How to Listen

Cary

SCHEDULING TIME FOR your own creative work and informing others of your progress often brings up deep emotion. It takes you by surprise, the strength of this emotion. You have laid yourself bare in an area you are not used to exposing to strangers, and it's delicate. Whether you are working one-on-one or leading a formal Finishing School workshop or are an attendee, you must be careful in what you say at such a moment.

Say you are leading a workshop and a person is just talking about a normal-sounding moment when she meant to work but for some reason was unable to get to it, and she goes silent and then starts weeping. What do you do? You listen. You let her weep. Maybe somebody hands her a tissue if there are copious tears. But we just let the moment happen. The best thing a workshop leader can do at a moment of intense emotion in the workshop is to listen and not offer suggestions but just listen and then keep listening and ask if there is anything else. If powerful emotions overtake a participant during the meeting, take time to let the person recover before moving on. It's okay. This is a deeply emotional process. We are talking about—if you want to get right down to it—recovering crucial, vital parts of who we are, often parts that have been neglected, so intense emotions arise when we realize that perhaps we have avoided catastrophe, that there is hope for the future, that we don't have to go to the grave never having achieved what we most fervently wanted to achieve. It's big stuff. It's normal to have big feelings about it. And it's normal to encounter emotional pain when we recount the ways that, in the past, we have turned away from or denigrated a sacred part of ourselves.

Listening carefully and fully when someone is experiencing deep emotion is hard to do, especially in a way that seems natural and not forced. Psychotherapists learn to do this kind of listening in their training. People in other helping professions learn it too. Perhaps for some deeply empathic and wise people it comes naturally. As for me, I learned to do this kind of listening in twelve-step meetings.

The basic fact is this: people need to be heard. We are in Finishing School to learn a method by which we can handle our own problems, and we will handle them ourselves, so we don't need advice particularly; we just need to be heard as we work through the process. Talking it through is crucial, but talking it through doesn't mean we're asking for suggestions. We are very vulnerable at such a moment, and the most well-intentioned suggestions can sound like critiques, as if we're not doing it right. Or they can jar us out of deep engagement into a more shallow social reality of reciprocity and politeness; we may feel that since someone offers a suggestion, even if it is a boneheaded one or inappropriate to our needs, we must thank them, and in thanking them we lend their suggestion credence even if it is inappropriate or useless. So we try not to just offer the first suggestion that comes to mind but to really hear, and feel, what the other person is experiencing.

The most we might offer at such a moment is a gentle question or two. Is there anything else? Are you ready to continue? Do you have a schedule for this week? Are there any barriers you see coming? Do you have a plan for what to do if these barriers arise?

We try to bring it back to the process, in which each of us is equally invested. This is exactly the opposite of what our instincts sometimes tell us to do at such a moment—that we must dig deeper into the person's problem, show interest in it.

In my vision for Finishing School, it is a set of methods that anyone can practice. We don't have to be experts in figuring out another person's psyche. That's not what we're there for. We respect the powerful emotions that arise, but we don't try to fix them. We simply hear them out completely, and then return to the program and keep moving on. I think this is the best way. It reminds us why we have come together. It reaffirms the dignity and vitality of our common purpose.

Have you ever read the poem "Aedh Wishes for the Cloths of Heaven" by William Butler Yeats? The last two lines describe such a moment nicely: "I have spread my dreams under your feet; / Tread softly because you tread on my dreams."

That's what a Finishing School workshop leader has to do: *tread softly because you tread on someone's dreams.*

Part 5

Finishing

John Steinbeck's Five Months in Finishing School

Danelle

IN 1938, WHEN John Steinbeck was writing the first draft of *The Grapes of Wrath*, he placed himself in his own version of Finishing School. Although Steinbeck had already written eight novels, including *Of Mice and Men*, *In Dubious Battle*, and *Tortilla Flat*, when he began *The Grapes of Wrath* he was certain he'd never written anything of value. He started work late in May, when a theatrical version of *Of Mice and Men* was about to start a successful Broadway run, but, as is recounted in *Working Days: The Journals of* The Grapes of Wrath, Steinbeck described his previous works as "makeshifts, experiments, practices." He felt that he must get one good book written before he died, and *The Grapes of Wrath* was his last chance. If he was not specific about what he wanted to write each day and did not hold himself accountable to the hours he had pledged to work, the book he was starting would slip away from him. He hoped the accountability created by his diary would keep him honest. "If a day is skipped it will show glaringly on this record and there will be some reason given for the slip," he writes on June 8, pledging to keep the diary going even if he starts to falter.

He worked in a small room in the Steinbeck home near Los Gatos, California, on the outer edge of what today is Silicon Valley. His office was just big enough for a bed, a desk, a bookshelf, and a gun rack. When he sat down at his desk, he took out his favorite fountain pen and noted the time of day he started, which was usually around 11:00 a.m., and what he intended to do that day—the equivalent of texting his creative buddy. His goal was ambitious: two thousand words a day, ten thousand a week, and he was merciless if he fell short of that mark.

As he labored under this pressure, his diary quickly evolved from a place to record those basic facts of his work to a chronicle of the things that threatened to keep him from finishing. This diary shows that he reacted to events outside his work solely from the point of view of whether or not they threatened his writing. This mono-focus made him prickly. Everyday noises, like the hammering from a neighbor's home remodel or the sound of the telephone or a distant radio, set him on edge. On a day when the washing machine seemed loud and he had a dentist appointment too, he wrote, "My whole nervous system is battered. I hope I am not headed for a nervous breakdown."

While he was quick to blame the outside world for getting in the way of his concentration, his sense of his own mediocrity also was a big distraction. "No one else knows my lack of ability the way I do," he wrote on June 18. "I am pushing against it all the time. Sometimes, I seem to do a good little piece of work, but when it is done it slides into mediocrity." At another point that month he praised the story and the people in it as so much greater than he was; he considered himself to be "small and inadequate and incapable."

Through his complaints, you also see how difficult it was to live with Steinbeck. If his wife, Carol, invited guests to dinner or for the weekend, he was always grumpy and often furious. Sometimes he threw guests out. When Carol got ill, Steinbeck was dutiful at first but got increasingly impatient as her disease lingered. In July he called the book "a prison term." Having a good time put him in a bad mood. One morning, hungover after a raucous dinner party, he wrote, "The failure of will even for one day has a devastating effect on the whole, far more important than just the loss of time and wordage. The whole physical basis of the novel is the discipline of the writer, of his material, of the language. And sadly enough, if any of the discipline is gone, all of it suffers." At one point he wrote that he wished he could just get away someplace remote until Christmas. He wrote that in August.

In that much misery, physically and emotionally, why do it? He did it because he sensed that he had been gifted with a great story and he saw himself as its servant, as if the story were passing through him and he had to do his best not to ruin it. "I'm afraid for this book," he wrote, as he listed his inadequacies. His entries were not all grim, as he recognized the days when he'd done well, but the bad days seemed to have more weight on his scale, and he was convinced that time was slipping away. "Now another week begins. . . . Empty feeling, empty show. . . . Terrible feeling of lost-ness and loneliness. . . . This book moves like a Tide Pool snail with a shell and barnacles on its back."

Reading his diary becomes comforting after a while, as it shows how deluded writing can make the writer. We may imagine that the great writers do not suffer the way lesser writers do. Maybe they did when they were working on their first books, but by the time they have one or two written most of those fears and insecurities had to have retreated, or so unpublished writers often believe. Yet here is John Steinbeck writing what will be one of the classic works of American literature, and his journal chronicles how even a writer at the apex of his talent and with more than a decade of experience is tortured with the same self-doubt, feelings of futility, and a frenzy to get some solitude that dogs any writer, experienced or not.

If you look at his diary from the framework of the Six Emotional Pitfalls, it is clear that Steinbeck suffered the most from shame, fear, and doubt. "I'm tired of the struggle against all the forces that this miserable success has brought against me. I don't know whether I could write a decent book now. That is the greatest fear of all. I'm working at it but I can't tell. Something is poisoned in me. You pages—ten of you—you are my dribble cup—you are the cloth to wipe up the vomit. Maybe I can get these fears and disgusts on you and then burn you up. Then maybe I won't be so haunted. . . . It is so hard to know anything. So impossible to trust oneself. Even to know what there is to trust. My will is low. I must build my will again."

He also has no sense of time. No matter how hard he works, he's always certain that he's behind and slipping even further, which is not true. He wrote the first draft of *The Grapes of Wrath* in five months.

Other emotional pitfalls do not bother him at all. He does not fear judgment because of his conviction that the rest of the world is foolish for thinking he is talented. In this way there is arrogance in his disdain of others' judgment because the only judgment that matters is his. The rest of the world is filled with fools who believe in him. He doesn't suffer from yearning for acclaim either, because his success embarrassed and harassed him. He believed he didn't deserve it and resented the additional demands it placed on his time. Some days he fantasized about how this book would rescue him from mediocrity, and others he welcomed its impending failure because once he lost it all, the noise around him would finally stop.

Through his version of Finishing School, Steinbeck kept writing, no matter how he felt about his work. The diary gave him a place to express these emotions so they didn't prevent him from finishing. As he neared the finish, the physical sensation made him believe he might not be able to make it to the end. "This blind weariness had me. I can't tell anyone about it but I am almost sick to my stomach with tiredness," he wrote on October 13, two weeks away from finishing.

The next day was tough too, and by the seventeenth he was drained of energy because he was unable to sleep. On the nineteenth, he confessed he didn't want to be done. "Strong reluctance to finish. Can't give myself the allowance of laziness just now. When it is done I can—but not until then. My mind doesn't want to work—hates to work in fact, but I'll make it. I'm on my very last chapter now. The very last. . . . I don't want this to seem hurried. It must be just as slow and measured as the rest but I am sure of one thing—it isn't the great book I had hoped it would be. It's just a run-of-the-mill book. And the awful thing is that it is absolutely the best I can do. Now to work on it."

The day before he finished, he was terrified and exhausted from lack of sleep, and on the day he was done he said he was so "dizzy I can hardly see the page." Reading that line, you wouldn't expect Steinbeck to finish it then, but he did, not with a feeling of triumph but with a whimper of doubt. "Finished this day—and I hope to God it's good." Steinbeck, the lifelong atheist, found himself so reduced by the labor of completing *The Grapes of Wrath* that he invoked God at the end.

Reading *Working Days* reminds us not to believe all those awful things we tell ourselves. Those feelings are not unique to us but, as Steinbeck shows, part of what we get when we try to do something that seems to be beyond the skills we use to live in the day-to-day world. To try something new is to court failure, but a focus on failure keeps us from getting down to work. Writing becomes not just the problem of what to write but the struggle against the writer's feeling of being unworthy. The way Steinbeck abuses himself for being lazy, mediocre, undisciplined, and a fraud sounds like the interior monologue of many writers we know and, on bad days, ourselves.

Steinbeck hacked his way through the thicket of his fears and just kept writing. He was distracted daily by the external world of demands on his time from strangers, from the run-up to World War II, and from his wife's demand that they sell the house and buy or build a newer, bigger one. At many points he decried the fact that no book was ever written under such terrible conditions. Then he remembered that his parents were dying during two of his previous books, and in earlier ones he didn't have the luxury of focusing solely on the writing because he had to make money. Conditions had actually been worse when he was writing earlier books. But the diary was a simple habit, like the habits of Finishing School, that kept him honest about his work. As he put it so well in August, when he was about halfway through: "Every book seems the struggle of a whole life. And then, when it is done—pouf. Never happened. Best thing is to get the words down every day."

The Completion High: What Finishing Feels Like

Danelle

As you approach the moment when you are about to place the final period on the page that contains the last sentence of work you really care about, your body fills with feeling. The week that John Steinbeck wrote the last chapter of *The Grapes of Wrath*, he recorded in his journal that his "nerves blew out like a fuse." He doubted the quality of his work and loathed the people who were about to judge it. His journal shows how finishing can land like a defeat, miring you in the feeling that you have not really finished—you just gave up. You ran out of hope, or you ran out of ideas, and anyway, you're not that good at this. As Steinbeck believed, you had not done your best, but you had nothing left to say. Finishing was not a triumph but a shameful abandonment of a dream.

In my work as a collaborator and a journalist, I've finished thousands of pieces. Cary wrote more than two thousand columns in the twelve years that he was an advice columnist for

Salon. For most of those, getting to the end has a workmanlike feeling, like sealing up a package. Writing the last sentence of a story about a city council meeting is a perfunctory act, as I know that as soon as I've completed that sentence I'll go back and check my work to see if any sentences can be shortened or if paragraphs or sentences should be shifted for better effect. One last sweep through, and off to the editor. That kind of finishing isn't emotional. I am finished, but need to finish again before sending. Writing something under difficult circumstances, like a tight deadline, or completing a piece that is personal and emotional, as with *The Grapes of Wrath*, is the kind of finishing that stays in the memory.

For one book collaboration I had an impossible eight-week deadline: six weeks for the first draft and two weeks for the second. When I wrote the last sentence of the second draft three days before the due date, I was having trouble keeping my fingers on the keys because I was driving hard toward the finish. I knew exactly where I was going and could not wait to get there. After the final period was on the screen, I yelled out in joy, stood up, and did a little goal-line dance. I was beaming, and I wished there were someone in the house to help me celebrate. Funny how during the eight weeks of intense focus on this deadline I was brusque with anyone who tried to take up my time, yet the minute when I was released from this thing, what I wanted most was human contact. I wanted to be hugged, toasted, carried around on someone's shoulders. I had done it. I had done this impossible thing and done it well. The book would go on to be a best seller.

In contrast to that, as I finished the story about the eight young people who died in a squat fire in New Orleans I sobbed. It had taken me a whole year to write those eight thousand words, and in doing so I thought again and again about the troubles my daughter and I had had. I questioned many of my actions and faced my regrets. I had interviewed fifty people who had lost loved ones in the fire, many of whom broke down crying when we spoke. The sobs I felt at the finish were not just for the lives lost, and the lives touched by that loss, but also for me and my daughter and what we had gone through as we walked the streets of New Orleans working on this story. It was finishing as a release, a release of loss and of grief as expressed in this piece that was so hard for me to complete. I felt proud, not just of myself, but proud of my daughter. Neither of us flinched.

WHEN CARY WROTE his advice column, it was due every weekday at 3:00 p.m. His criteria for completion were that he had offered something useful to the reader in trouble and done so in a fresh and unexpected way. The standard was heartfelt, but it was also important to be entertaining as well as to give the problem the letter writer had offered a complete exploration. Had he put himself in the writer's shoes? If he had managed to do all those things by 3:00, then he was done for the day.

Every now and then he would experience something rare, a kind of high, a mystical experience of communion and having hit on the right combination of words to express the depth and complexity of the situation. When that happened, he is embarrassed to say, he would cry. Just as with my ecstatic finishing experience, he knew when tears arose as he was finishing that he had touched something beyond the usual.

———

So those are the high moments, but the truth is, finishing does not always seem like a worthwhile goal. There's a whole different emotional tone to the sentence "You're finished in this town." You're tossed out on your ass, never to write again. This thing you wrote is so bad, someone is coming to confiscate your pencil case and torch your notebooks; an edict has been issued from a high court compelling you to confine your writing to e-mails. You're done.

Or you may avoid finishing because you fear trying to sell your book. You dread calling up editors or trying to get an agent. You know that you are not very thick skinned and that people are busy. They may be rude to you, or ignore your repeated requests for contact, which can only validate your feelings of worthlessness. Or being ignored may enrage you, and you might pout and be cranky to those you love because the fact that no one will pay attention to you makes you mad at the world. If you get an editor or an agent to read what you've finished, they may reject it or return a harsh critique. Those words sting, and the wounds may take awhile to heal. If the work never finds a sympathetic audience, will you continue to write? There is no way of knowing. So finishing may truly be the end, which is why many people sputter out of motivation right as they reach the finish.

What's good about completing your work in Finishing School is that it takes the drama away from finishing. The act of finishing becomes a habit. You finish something every week, and each time you do you set down a new goal to fulfill the next week. Finishing becomes a familiar experience, and the more you finish, the faster you get at knowing when something is complete. Being in the habit of finishing helps you handle the fear of what awaits you on that exceptional day when you can say that you are done.

We trust that you will know when you are finished. We trust that you will feel it, just as we have. The habit of finishing small pieces week by week will build your sense of confidence in your work, and when you reach the real finish line, there will be no mistaking the feeling that you struggled, you sweated, you wrestled and avoided, but in the end you finished and it feels great.

Finishing Well, No Matter How It Ends

Danelle

Sometimes the problem with finishing is knowing when to quit.

It feels bad when you quit on a dream, but the dream might be the wrong one. Not to say that it is wrong to dream, just that some of our dreams do not age well.

I dreamed of being an astronaut when I was six, but it was a career ill suited to a person who, like me, is short and not that good at math. I didn't know that I would grow up to have either of those deficiencies when I imagined floating on a tether through space. My dream was of an ecstatic experience, not the preceding years of science, physical fitness, math, and rigorous training. This is where some imaginations go when people think about finishing their books. The book might as well be floating on a tether in space.

You might dream of writing a book and find out that you do not like to write. All writers at some point loathe the process.

As Dorothy Parker said, "I hate writing. I love having written." If you find the work unbearable, there is no reason to continue not having fun with your creative side.

Maybe life has thrown you out of sync with your writing if you pick it up after a long absence. Say you started an autobiographical novel when you were just out of college and then return to it a decade later. You're a different person now, and some of the things you were trying to figure out then you have now decided. The question at the center of the novel now seems like a dumb one. The person on the page still is you, but you cannot conjure that voice.

Perhaps the idea came to you during a period of excess that's long past, and you just can't tell that story anymore. Or, upon close examination, maybe the story is not as it seemed at first. The plot is not as good as you had imagined, and when you straighten out that problem, the ending is all wrong.

When you think about this project, you feel hopeless, but it seems a shame to leave behind all those completed pages. This dream of finishing your book, of being published, is one that you have never let loose of. To walk away from this project may make you think you are weak or lazy, someone who will never amount to much because you don't have what it takes to fulfill your dream. Having this dream and not accomplishing it makes you feel like the dream is judging you.

There is no shame in abandoning a project whose problems have become impossible, as long as you know you gave it your all. If finishing this project is something you really want to do, you have to go after it with everything you have within you. If there are skills you need to learn, learn them. Read and remember the things you admire about other writers. Work on expanding your imagination and finding ways to describe the things you see from a point of view, and in a language, of your own. Keep your eyes open as you walk down the street to spot a quirk of carriage or tilt of the hat that might be useful to you in your book. Listen to the way people talk, their malapropisms and their accents, and jot them down. Look at the world as a novel, and choose the world of your novel from that. Put in the hours in the chair, wrestling with the prose and wrestling with the pitfalls.

And after you've tried to stretch yourself in all these ways and to open to all that you can see and most of what you can feel, then you decide if you want to finish. That way, it does not finish you.

You gave it a try, and a good one. It didn't end up being the thing you dreamed of, so it's time to pick a new dream. Time to adjust the dream to the dreamer. There is no shame in that. Everything you did to finish your novel helped you engage more with your world. You're not done yet. Dream a new dream and go after that one.

The Detailed Scenario
of Doneness

Cary

You know you have to stop working on your project eventually and call it done, right?

But how? How do you know when the work is done?

Well, you create a "detailed scenario of doneness." You identify the steps you need to take to consider the project done. And then you take them. You tick them off. It's that simple. Whether you complete these tasks brilliantly or only moderately well, they are the finishing touches that indicate that you have done what you need to do and are ready to move on.

So. What does a detailed scenario of doneness look like?

It looks like a to-do list in the form of affirmations. Say you wanted to create a detailed scenario of doneness for a long magazine article. It's a portrait of how you want the thing to be and how you want to feel about it.

- I have written a compelling lead that I'm happy with.
- I have checked all direct quotes with my tapes to make sure they are accurate.
- When necessary, I have had subjects read their quotes to make sure they are accurate.
- I have gone through the piece and removed extraneous paragraphs that don't advance the central story.
- I have ensured that the voice is consistent.
- I have checked the spellings of all place names.
- I have checked the spellings of the names of all persons.
- I have written an ending that I'm happy with.
- There are no sentences that are unbearably awkward.
- There are no statements that are potentially libelous.
- It has a good headline.

That's just an example. In Finishing School most projects are longer. They are nonfiction books, screenplays, poetry collections, and novels. A detailed scenario of doneness for a novel might look something like this:

- I have a title for the novel that I love.
- My opening scene is engaging, displays my skill as a writer, and is an appropriate lead-in to the novel itself.
- I love everything about it.
- I feel good about the ending.
- I'm glad I wrote it.
- I know not everything in it is totally brilliant, but at the same time there is nothing outright stupid in it, or ludicrous or false in the aesthetic sense.

- It has one or two parts I think are really funny.
- My main character is consistent in voice and appearance, and she does evolve and change.
- There is a story line.
- In Jane Smiley's formulation, I know it is a novel because it is a long written prose narrative with a protagonist.

Et cetera. Each work will of course have a unique detailed scenario of doneness.

Let's take one more example that names some material conditions that signify you are done with this work and it is ready:

- I have a manuscript that is clean, in professional format, and free of grammatical mistakes and typographical eros (that's a joke).
- I'm happy with the piece and ready to have somebody else see it.
- I have read through the entire manuscript and there is nothing in it that makes me cringe.
- I have spent as much time on it as I had planned for.

You will of course have more conditions. Some conditions may be private. For instance, in order to be happy with this project, you may want to include a particular terrifying or gripping scene, or a couple of really amazing sentences that make you unequivocally happy, no matter what anybody else says. You could put that in as a condition:

- On page 43, there's that description of an apple tree I like so much.

- I have one scene that is so gripping and wonderful it makes me happy that it's in the manuscript.

The point is to create a list that makes you happy. You can use it as a checklist as you move steadily toward being finished. And if it is a scenario that makes you happy when you think about it, then it will also work to motivate you to continue. You can tack it up on your wall. It might function as a kind of affirmation, if you're into that sort of thing.

Creating such a list of course raises questions about quality and perfection and aesthetic value. But Finishing School is not a method for establishing aesthetic value. It is a method that allows a writer to put aside those questions and focus on tangible, incremental progress.

Like you, I want to write enormously complex and engaging work. I just know that I will never get this amazingly complex, difficult, challenging work done if I do not have a set of concrete steps to follow.

I just need a path. And you do too. So please do not put this book down because it seems to disregard the complexity and mystery of the writing process. Please think of it more as a mundane but necessary tool, like a desk or a chair, something that supports your corporeal being while your mind performs magical activities. Think of it as a method that helps you get the work done, so you can take the next step and write your Declaration of Done.

Conclusion:
The Declaration of Done

Cary

When all the conditions spelled out in the detailed scenario of doneness are met, it is time to make your Declaration of Done.

You might put it something like this:

I, [Jane Doe], hereby certify and solemnly swear that I am done with this work, and therefore, after this date, I pledge to make no more corrections, insertions, or revisions to this manuscript.

By simple fiat, like the king of France, you declare that you are done with this manuscript.

You could stop there. The joy of being finished is yours. You could take some time off. Maybe go to France, where they had all those kings who would declare things by fiat.

But it's more likely that this is just the first step. If you are interested in offering it for publication somewhere, then continue as follows:

> **My next step after this date is to submit the manuscript to professionals for review, for the ultimate purpose of publication. I promise to keep my grubby hands off it until it has been submitted and I have waited a sufficient amount of time to hear back.**
>
> **Furthermore, unless and until I receive from a publishing professional concrete instructions for revisions that might plausibly lead to publication, I will not look at it again. I will not tinker. I will not reconsider. I will not rephrase, check spelling, consider a better way to say something, write an alternate ending, change characters' names, change locations, or alter anything else. I pledge to let the goddamned manuscript alone.**

Now, offering a work for publication often involves excerpting material. This allows people who cannot read the entire thing to just get a sense of it. Often such a person will ask for the first fifty pages. It is tempting when that happens (I know from experience) to go and tinker with the first fifty pages, thinking you have to get these first fifty pages especially right. Don't do it.

Instead, include something like this in your Declaration of Done:

> **I have already excerpted the first fifty pages to supply to any interested party if asked, so I need not be tempted to go in and alter those. The first fifty pages**

**are the first fifty pages exactly as they appear in the
entire work.**

The same would apply if an agent asked for the first three
chapters or the first ten pages or whatever. Make a pledge to
send exactly what they ask for, without changes.

Further:

**After submission, I promise not to change anything
except and until a credible publishing professional
makes a convincing argument for why such changes
would make the manuscript salable. I will accept no
vague suggestions like "the main character needs to
be stronger"; I pledge to act only on clear, concrete,
specific, executable suggestions. If I agree to make
such changes, I will submit them by a mutually agreed
deadline.**

**This Declaration of Done is certified and signed
this date, by me, the creator of this work.**

That's it. You've now declared you are done.

Notice we do not focus on questions of quality, like when it
is *good enough*. Good enough is one of those vague, potentially
disastrous notions that get into your head and drive you crazy.
Good enough. Sheesh.

Finishing School is about freeing you from the torment of
not knowing if you will ever escape this cycle of invention and
revision that you are trapped in. Finishing School is a method
for reaching a state of completion and moving on.

It takes on the fantastically complex issue of an aesthetic or intellectual work with a deliberately simplified attitude. That's the whole point. Your thoughts can be as complex and compelling as you want them to be. In your day-to-day practice of craft, however, it pays to take the route of the possible.

We ask: When will you be finished with the work? What concrete steps are you going to take?

Why? So your genius can flower.

If you enjoyed this book, visit

www.tarcherperigee.com

and sign up for TarcherPerigee's e-newsletter to receive special offers, updates on hot new releases, and articles containing the information you need to live the life you want.

tarcherperigee

LEARN. CREATE. GROW.

Connect with the TarcherPerigee Community

. . .

Stay in touch with favorite authors

Enter giveaway promotions

Read exclusive excerpts

Voice your opinions

Follow us

TarcherPerigee

@TarcherPerigee

@TarcherPerigee

If you would like to place a bulk order of this book,
call 1-800-733-3000.